AUSTRA]
Expeditiona1

—

RECRUITS W

CW01507946

—

Every Man Physically Fit is Wanted.

—

CONDITIONS OF ENLISTMENT.

Age... ...   ...18 to 45 years.

Minimum Height...   ...5 feet 2 inches.

Chest Measurement   ...33 inches.

Persons desiring to enlist should apply at the nearest Town Hall, Shire Hall, Drill Hall, or Recruiting Depot, where arrangements will be made for medical examination.

Persons who are considered suitable will be granted Free Railway Tickets to the Metropolis for final medical examination and enlistment.

RATES OF PAY PER DAY.

	On and from date
	Prior to	of embarkation
	embarkation.	(including deferred pay).
Lieutenant	... 15/	... 21/
Sergeant...	... 10/	... 10/6
Corporal...	... 9/	... 10/
Private ...	... 5/	... 6/

SEPARATION ALLOWANCE.

Separation allowance will be paid to married men who are receiving less than 8/ per day, but such allowance will not exceed the amount necessary to make up the difference between their daily rate of pay and 8/ per day.

Subject to this limitation the amounts payable are as follows :—(a) For wife living at home, 1/5 per day. (b) For each child under 16 years of age, 4½d per day.

A similar allowance as in (a) is payable under the same conditions to the mother of a member, if she is solely dependent on him for support.

PENSIONS.

Pensions payable to a widow on death of member of the Forces or to a member on total incapacity—

Lieutenant	...	...	£91 per annum.
Sergeant	...	...	£70 " "
Corporal	...	...	£68 " "
Private	...	...	£52 " "

In addition, on the death or total incapacity of a member, for each child under 16 years of age, £13 per annum.

In cases of total incapacity, the wife in addition receives half the rate specified above for the respective rank.

Pensions are payable also to other dependents.

FROM GALLIPOLI WITH LOVE

Dear Mother,

FLORENCE BREED

ABOUT THE AUTHOR

Florence Breed lives in Donald, Victoria. An active local historian, she hails from Cornish stock and is the author of *A Devonshire lad : from Mullacott to Jeffcott*, *Woodbine wives from World War I*, *Forgotten heroes of the South African war 1899–1902* and *Old Cornish Tales*.

Published in Australia by Sid Harta Publishers Pty Ltd,

ABN: 34 632 585 203

17 Coleman Parade, GLEN WAVERLEY VIC 3150 Australia

Telephone: +61 3 9560 9920, Facsimile: +61 3 9545 1742

E-mail: author@sidharta.com.au

First published in Australia 2020

This edition published 2020

Copyright © Florence Breed 2020

Cover design, typesetting: WorkingType (www.workingtype.com.au)

Breed, Florence

From Gallipoli with Love

ISBN: 978-1-925707-35-9

pp346

Cover Photo — Private Alfred Bailes, of Donald.

CONTENTS

AUSTRALIAN
Expeditionary Forces

RECRUITS WANTED.

Every Man Physically Fit is Wanted.

CONDITIONS OF ENLISTMENT.

Age ...	...	18 to 45 years.
Minimum Height...	...	5 feet 2 inches.
Chest Measurement	...	33 inches.

Persons desiring to enlist should apply at the nearest Town Hall, Shire Hall, Drill Hall, or Recruiting Depot, where arrangements will be made for medical examination.

Persons who are considered suitable will be granted Free Railway Tickets to the Metropolis for final medical examination and enlistment.

RATES OF PAY PER DAY.

		Prior to embarkation.		On and from date of embarkation (including deferred pay).
Lieutenant	...	15/	...	21/
Sergeant...	...	10/	...	10/6
Corporal...	...	9/	...	10/
Private ...	...	5/	...	6/

SEPARATION ALLOWANCE.

Separation allowance will be paid to married men who are receiving less than 8/ per day, but such allowance will not exceed the amount necessary to make up the difference between their daily rate of pay and 8/ per day.

Subject to this limitation the amounts payable are as follows :—(a) For wife living at home, 1/5 per day. (b) For each child under 16 years of age, 4½d per day.

A similar allowance as in (a) is payable under the same conditions to the mother of a member, if she is solely dependent on him for support.

PENSIONS.

Pensions payable to a widow on death of member of the Forces or to a member on total incapacity—

Lieutenant	...	...	£91 per annum.
Sergeant	...	...	£70 ,, ,,
Corporal	...	...	£68 ,, ,,
Private	...	...	£52 ,, ,,

In addition, on the death or total incapacity of a member, for each child under 16 years of age, £13 per annum.

In cases of total incapacity, the wife in addition receives half the rate specified above for the respective rank.

Pensions are payable also to other dependents.

Cover Photo - Private Alfred Bailes, of Donald.

GALLIPOLI

The campaign to capture the Gallipoli peninsula was part of the British government's strategy against Germany. Winston Churchill, who was First Sea Lord at that time, wanted the Allies to conquer Turkey, a strong ally of Germany. Thus, the Allied Forces could invade Europe through the back door and so attack Germany from the east as well as from the west.

At the beginning of 1915, Churchill had ordered an attack by sea against Constantinople which had failed, so now his plan was to attack on land. He hoped British and Allied forces could capture the western shore of the Gallipoli peninsula and then advance up the peninsula to capture the capital city of Turkey (now known as Istanbul).

But Churchill had not realized there were strong defences in the south of Gallipoli where the British and French forces landed — and he was not aware of the terrible high cliffs where the Anzac forces landed as they were far too steep for an invasion.

Unaware that thousands of Turks were entrenched in the hills above them, it soon became impossible for the Anzacs to climb those cliffs and penetrate further inland to capture the Gallipoli peninsula.

Before the end of the year they would have to withdraw, leaving the bits of ground they had managed to win, but worst of all they had to leave behind their comrades, buried there for ever.

(1865 — 1936)

King George V came to the throne of England in 1910. This gentle-mannered king and his consort, Queen Mary, were the most democratic of monarchs to ever rule England. They were much-loved for their kindliness and straight-forward patriotism. During the Great War, both King and Queen worked for the good of their subjects. He visited war-zones to inspire the fighting men; and both went into hospitals to console the sick and wounded.

This evil man escaped punishments at the end of the war and
ran away to hide in the Netherlands.
He stole German money and lived in comfort to an old age.

King George V (1865–1936)
Queen Mary (d. 1953)

THE GERMAN EMPEROR

Here, King Wilhelm haughtily-poses in the uniform of the famous Death's Head Hussars.

He was a bully and brutally-ambitious; and it is possible that the history of the world would have been very different had his father lived longer. Kaiser Frederick was a kind and gentle man, who died from cancer of the throat at an early age.

This evil man escaped punishment at the end of the war and ran away to hide in the Netherlands.

He stole German money and lived in comfort to an old age.

ASSASSINATION OF THE ARCHDUKE

The First World War began in August, 1914, and if we want to blame one person for lighting the fuse that started this massacre we could name a fanatical 19-year old terrorist called Gavrilo Princip. He was a Bosnian Serb who pumped bullets into the Archduke Ferdinand, and his wife, Sophie, as their car passed him on the streets of Sarajevo. It was June 28th. and both his victims died within minutes.

Most historians agree it was those two bullets from a terrorist's gun that triggered the war — resulting in four years of slaughter and suffering as Europe blew itself to pieces.

"Enlist! Enlist!" said Kitchener, to each Australian son;
"Your Empire needs you now to fight against the brutal Hun.
Come, gallant lads, and join the fight to help us win the war,
And you shall earn the gratitude and thanks from rich and poor."

A REMINDER

This book tells the most compelling story in the history of Australia and New Zealand; yet for such an important story, nobody really claims to know everything about it.

Perhaps we think we do; and if you ask the question, "Have you heard of Gallipoli?" I'm sure every hand would go up.

But if you asked where was it, and why was it, and why we were fighting the Turks, those hands would go down rapidly.

As soon as you study the following accounts found in the dairies and letters of Australian soldiers, the whole story becomes a personal experience for you — and a strong link with the men who were there.

Their writings give vivid accounts of the battles that took place on the Peninsula in 1915 between allied and Turkish troops; and also give to us some inkling of the disastrous decisions made by allied commanders that led to the pointless killing or maiming of 27,000 Australians.

BRITAIN DECLARED WAR ON GERMANY

BRITAIN DECLARED WAR
ON GERMANY

7ᵗʰ. Infantry Battalion (Victorian) on the March

PRESENT FROM A PRINCESS

Princess Mary was the only daughter of King George V and Queen Mary. She was training as a nurse in Guy's Hospital, London, and therefore personally witnessed the great numbers of wounded soldiers arriving from the battlefields of France. The Great War started in 1914 and was not going well for our soldiers during those first months, especially during the retreat from Mons when there was a heavy loss of life.

Consequently, Princess Mary had the idea of giving a Christmas present to all those men who were fighting for Britain against the evil German Kaiser. She decided that those on active service needed a little extra in the way of home comforts now the festive season was approaching.

So the "Princess Mary's Sailors' and Soldiers' Christmas Fund" was launched in October, 1914, in which she appealed to the public for Christmas gifts to be sent to the soldiers at the battlefront on December 25th.

She became the head of a committee which would decide on the best ways to raise the cash — and consequently the appeal resulted in the magnificent total of over 162,591 pounds. Collections came from churches, schools and industries and from concerts and entertainments — as well as from boxes that were placed on shop counters.

It was such a generous response from the public that it was decided that every man wearing the King's uniform on Christmas Day should receive a gift. This included members of the Army and Navy, prisoners-of-war and Colonial troops — as well as nurses and the next-of-kin of the fallen.

IX

Princess
Mary

(died 1965)

This Christmas gift would be a brass box (5in.× 3in) containing either cigarettes or chocolates (for smoker or non-smokers) and on the lid the profile of Princess Mary and the date (Christmas 1914). On the surrounds there were the names of our allies: Serbia, Japan, France, Russia, Belgium and Montenegro.

Princess Mary
(died 1965)

TERRORISM – OVER A CENTURY AGO IN AUSTRALIA

It was in 1915, on New Year's Day, that several people were killed in an act of terrorism at Broken Hill, in New South Wales — and, unfortunately, this true story has become lost in the mists of time.

It happened one peaceful summer's day when the local branch of the Unity Order of Oddfellows and their families set out early in the morning to enjoy an annual picnic. They travelled into the countryside along the Silverton tramway and were seated in open trucks.

Hostile Fire. The train had only travelled about two miles down the line when those on board noticed a strange sight beside the track ahead. An ice-cream cart was flying a strange black flag — a Turkish one it later turned out to be — and near it stood two men who appeared to be Asians. They had guns and seemed to be shooting at rabbits. Then, in disbelief, the people on the train suddenly began to realize that those two men were actually firing at their trucks.

Almost immediately after the shooting began, five people died — a young man, an elderly woman, a girl and a boy and also a man on horseback who had been riding beside the train.

After the trucks had passed beyond the point of ambush, a message was quickly sent back to Broken Hill and soon a contingent of police and soldiers arrived at the scene. But in the meantime, the two gunmen had gone to a nearby cottage and after killing its two occupants made suitable preparations inside the hut for their inevitable confrontation with the Law.

They must have known that their actions were suicidal and doomed from the beginning. For some time the police and gunmen exchanged shots until one of the gunmen was killed and the other mortally-wounded. The

The Manchester Unity picnic train attacked by 'Turks' at Broken Hill on New Year's Day

killers were later found to be an Afghan and a Turk. In fact, one of them was a well-known local butcher and the other was a travelling ice-cream seller.

Misplaced Patriotism. Now, we know it was in August, 1914, at the beginning of the First World War, that Turkey made an alliance with Germany to support the fight against Britain and her allies. As for Afghanistan, Britain had already fought two wars against that country in the 1800's — so it appears that these two lone representatives of their different countries had decided to fight in faraway Australia which they considered to be an enemy power.

As a result of that suicidal act of terrorism, seven innocent citizens lost their lives — and to what end? It was later proved that the idea to murder people was entirely their own and that no one else and no other country was implicated.

Retaliation. Of course, the local people who had loved ones and friends killed in that shooting attack, wanted to retaliate, and, therefore taking the law into their own hands, proceeded to burn down the German Club in Broken Hill.

An attack upon a camp of Afghan camel-drivers was also

planned — but the police were able to prevent such lawlessness by proving that no one else was involved in that terrible act of terrorism and that the two murderers had acted alone.

Perhaps the lesson to be learnt from this event in Australia at the beginning of the First World War is that we should not blame <u>all</u> people just because they have the same religion as fanatics who commit mad and murderous deeds.

ZEPPELIN RAIDS ON ENGLAND

In August, 1914, Germany (with Austria-Hungary) declared war upon Great Britain, France and Belgium; and just a few months later that cunning enemy became the first country in the history of Mankind to drop deadly missiles from the air upon helpless, innocent civilians. Huge airships (known as ZEPPELINS and carrying deadly weapons of destruction) soon began to float above England's coastal areas.

On the 19th of January, 1915, the very first German bombs fell upon England at Yarmouth and King's Lynn with the tragic result that four people were killed and nine injured — one bomb even fell upon the King's holiday home (Sandringham House) although no harm was done to the royal family. Zeppelins flew over the south coast again on 21st. February, dropping their bombs upon Colchester and Braintree, yet thankfully no one was hurt that time.

On the 14th of April, Zeppelins attacked Blyth and Wallsend when only two people were injured — and two days later several bombs fell upon Lowestoft, Ipswich and Bury St. Edmunds without any injury to life, or property. At the beginning of May, four Zeppelins flew over Southend, Westcliff and Leigh — and this time the death toll was a woman and her canary.

Succeeding visits of these great airships grew more serious and when Ramsgate was next visited, eight people were injured and two killed. At Southend on May 27th. two women and a young girl were killed.

People used to rush into the streets to watch the great

Zeppelins slowly floating overhead, but later the public was warned to stay indoors because there was more to fear from falling British shells than from enemy bombs. Several people were killed in this way after being struck by a piece of shrapnel as they stood in the streets staring up at the sky.

IS **YOUR** HOME WORTH FIGHTING FOR?

IT WILL BE TOO LATE TO FIGHT WHEN THE ENEMY IS AT YOUR DOOR

SO JOIN TO-DAY

On the night of May 31st. it was London's turn; and this Zeppelin raid was a great shock to Londoners who firmly believed the floating, enemy airships were too slow and ungainly to escape the gunnery fortifications stationed all along the River Thames. However, one great Zeppelin did manage to fly over Britain's capital city and dropped a large number of bombs which killed six people and destroyed many buildings. It was this air-raid that caused major riots in the city because angry Londoners began to attack and destroy German-owned shops.

About this time, public feelings in Britain were also badly inflamed by the sinking of the passenger ship, *Lusitania*; and folks talked about this murderous act for years afterwards. That great liner was steaming off the coast of Ireland on the 7th. May, 1915, when a German U-boat fired a single torpedo into her side, ripping the *Lusitania* apart. The huge passenger ship sank to the bottom of the ocean in just eighteen minutes and all of the 1198 people on board were killed. (It was this senseless tragedy that started to inflame anti-German feelings in America and led to that country joining the Allies later in the war.)

More serious Air-Raids occurred over England's North-East coast in June and July with a total of twenty people killed and fifty-five injured; and Air-raids also occurred in August, killing and injuring many more people.

Now, the majority of victims in Zeppelin raids were innocent women and children, so how exactly did the enemy benefit from its callous actions? What did the Germans hope to achieve by such unnecessary, civilian slaughter?

THE END OF A ZEPPELIN

The recent destruction of a huge, German Zeppelin, L15, proves that British air-defences are successfully protecting these shores from murderers who attack innocent women and children. Fortunately for the vicious raiders, the crippled Zeppelin did not crash upon land, but fell slowly into the River Thames where the 18 Germans were rescued and made prisoners by a passing trawler. Shortly afterwards, the wrecked Zeppelin broke in two and sank to the bottom of the river.

TRUCE IN THE TRENCHES

(By Florence Breed)

"Goodwill to men and Peace on earth!" sang Heavenly Choirs
On Christmas Day, one hundred years ago —
So the killing stopped, blood ceased to flow,
Each soldier stood up in his trench and waved to the foe.
It was silent that day, only birds in the sky.
No screaming bullets to cause endless pain,
No shrieking shells to smash a man's brain,
Only clouds floated by with a promise of rain.
The singing of carols and feelings of brotherhood
Turned No-Man's Land into a joyful place,
Where games were played and our soldiers chase
The Hun, enjoying the fun, with smiles on every face.
Then, as the skies of night arrive on silent wings
Above that torn and tortured earth, each man disappears,
Invisible in the shadows, returning to the fears
That break of dawn will once again bring Death with many tears.

A Christmas Miracle

NOT A LEGEND

The truce on Christmas Day in 1914 during World War I was often thought of as a pleasant legend.

The following extract from "The Fifth Battalion, The Cameronians (Scottish Rifles) 1914-1919" proves that it was a real and happy event:

"On Christmas Eve we could hear the Germans (XIXth Saxon Corps) celebrating the advent of Christmas by singing and merrymaking. We could also hear a brass band behind the houses in their lines playing Christmas carols.

"For roughly twenty-four hours, Christmas Eve to late afternoon on Christmas Day, they ceased firing at us, and we reciprocated.

"An attempt at fraternization took place on Christmas Day, 'Jerry' leaving his trench unarmed. Certain souvenirs were exchanged and, if it had been left to the soldiery of both sides, the war would then and there have been declared a draw.

"But towards late afternoon on Christmas Day a stray shot from on our right front hit one of ours, No. 6179, Corpl. W.S. Smith, No. 2 Company, from which he died next day.

"The Saxons opposite us were at pains to let us know that it was a Prussian who had fired the shot which killed Smith. This broke the spell, however, and the war was resumed after a tacit truce of twenty-four hours.

"This truce drew forth an army routine order reminding us that we were in France to fight and not to fraternize with the enemy."

THE ILL-FATED CUNARD LINER "LUSITANIA."

TORPEDOED AND SUNK BY GERMAN SUBMARINE OFF THE OLD HEAD OF KINSALE, IRELAND

THE ILL-FATED CUNARD LINER "LUSITANIA."
TORPEDOED AND SUNK BY GERMAN SUBMARINE OFF THE OLD HEAD OF KINSALE, IRELAND.
MAY 7TH, 1915.

MAY 7TH, 1915.
FOVANT TRAINING CAMP – ON SALISBURY PLAIN, ENGLAND – 1914

There's an isolated, desolated spot I'd like to mention,
Where all you hear is, "Stand at ease", "Slope Arms",
"Quick March", "Attention".
It's miles away from anywhere, by gad it is a rum 'un.
Chaps could live here for forty years and never see a woman.
There are lots of little huts, all dotted here and there,
For those who have to live inside, I've offered many a prayer.
Inside the huts there's RATS as big as any nanny goat,
Last night a soldier saw one trying on his overcoat.
It's mud up to the eyebrows, you get it in your ear,
But into it you've got to go without a sign of fear.
And when you've had a bath of mud you just set to and groom,
And get cleaned up for next Parade, or else it's "Orderly Room".
Week in, week out, from morn till night, with full Pack and a Rifle,
Like Jack and Jill you climb the hill, of course that's just a trifle.
"Slope Arms", "Fix Bayonets", then "Present", they fairly put you through it,
And as you stagger to your Hut, the Sergeant shouts, "Jump to it".
With tunics, boots and putties off, you quickly get the habit,
You gallop up and down the hills just like a blooming rabbit.
"Heads backward bend", "Arms stretch", "Heels raise", "All change places".
And later on they make you put your kneecaps where your face is.
Now when this War is over and we've captured Kaiser Billy,
To shoot him would be merciful and absolutely silly.

xxx

Just send him down to Fovant Camp among the Rats and Clay,
I bet it wouldn't be long before he droops and fades away.
(by an anonymous soldier)

IN PRAISE OF OUR SOLDIERS

It was the soldier, not the poet.
Gave us freedom of expression.
'Twas the soldier, not the preacher,
Gave us freedom of religion.
'Twas the soldier, not Trade Unions,
Gave us better work conditions.
And 'twas the soldier made this country free,
Not party politicians.
Freedom from Want, Freedom from Fear,
And Freedom of Speech which we hold dear.
'Lest We Forget' are words we say
When marching every Anzac Day.
So keep alight that undying flame
To honour those who deserve great fame.

F.B.

WEAPONS OF THE
FIRST WORLD WAR

The Lee Enfield a 1 ft 60 ins long bayonet.

The Lee Enfield .303 bore rifle. It was the standard rifle for all Commonwealth troops.

The Vickers machine gun. It was capable of rapid, widespread fire which made it a deadly weapon against massed enemy infantry. The Vickers was water-cooled. It could fire a belt of 500 rounds per minute.

1914: Australia sent 20,000 men to war

Fall-in!

"AUSTRALIA WILL BE THERE!"

(Skipper Francis)

Here is the Chorus of that popular song which was sung by Australian soldiers everywhere in the First World War. These words were sung (probably shouted) by them, with great gusto and patriotic fervour, in times of danger and fighting. Our men were proud of their Homeland, and woe betide any German or Turk who threatened it. Even after the war, this song was still sung — and almost became a National Anthem. People sang it as a tribute to the Anzacs of Gallipoli and the Diggers of France.

DEPARTURE OF THE
VICTORIAN CONTINGENT

Australian troops were destined for Egypt.

"Enlist! Enlist!" said Kitchener, to each Australian son;
"Your Empire needs you now to fight against the brutal Hun.
Come, gallant lads, and join the fight to help us win the war,
And you shall earn the gratitude and thanks from rich and poor."

Here are letters written by the soldiers while on active duty at the front line, to their parents, families and/or friends; and there are extracts from the diaries of Sgt. Alexander Walder and Sgt. Arthur Clifford.

These writings are first hand impressions and experiences on the front line, written by the soldiers themselves. They tell of the hardships they had to endure, such as the cold, wet and muddy conditions. The roads were described as "thick sticky porridge", and the trenches, "when we got into them, we were up to our waists in mud".

They also tell of the suicidal bayonet charges that took place towards the enemy trenches.

The diary of Sgt. Alexander Walder:—

"As for our boys, they are just splendid. They are looked up to as the best fighting troops of the world — an honour they have won by their gallant and ever ready devotion to duty in the face of all dangers. And if they fall, remember that no greater love hath any man"

xl

THE IMMORTAL LANDING

Sent to Egypt instead of Britain — because of the shortage of suitable accommodation there — the AIF spent some months in Egypt training on the desert sands just outside Cairo and beneath the shadow of the pyramids.

Their first campaign was at Gallipoli against Turkey who was Germany's ally. Of course, our soldiers would rather have been fighting the Germans themselves. However, with the British soldiers they then became part of the Mediterranean Expeditionary Force under the command of General Sir Ian Hamilton.

Their courageous landing on Gallipoli's shores on the 25th. April, in 1915, beneath the fury of enemy guns firing down on them from the cliffs above, proved that those men of the AIF were amongst the best fighters.

Sadly, their eight-month campaign failed entirely to achieve its purpose, but the men of those Australian and New Zealand troops at ANZAC Cove demonstrated extraordinary courage, stamina and endurance.

We can blame the terrible weather conditions they had to face that winter, but also some incompetence at a higher level.

The most successful feature of that campaign [which cost the AIF over 8,000 dead and 18,000 wounded,] was the evacuation in December, planned by Colonel C.B.B.White, when the Australians withdrew without suffering a single casualty.

INTRODUCTION

We know that over 8000 Australians died in the Gallipoli Campaign of 1915 and I wish to pay homage to all of them. However, this collection of writings especially honours those soldiers who went to fight in the Great War from our particular area of Victoria known as the Wimmera, for it was the children of these men who kindly gave me permission to publish some of the following material. I was grateful for the opportunity to see war-diaries, photos, viewcards and letters that had been lovingly preserved for almost 100 years.

I found in all the soldiers' writings that famous quality of character which is called the "ANZAC SPIRIT" and I believe that today's young people should be made aware of its significance to the history of our country.

After studying these letters and diaries, I came to the conclusion that this invisible "ANZAC SPIRIT" consists of — (1) an unquenchable fire of adventure combined with an unbreakable spirit in times of adversity; (2) a wonderful tenacity of purpose which made our Anzacs extremely bold and daring when facing great odds; (3) a burning love for Australia and their Motherland; and, last but not least, (4) a keenness which made them rush to arms at the first sound of war, caring for nothing but to get into the thick of it at the earliest possible moment.

An amazing fact to me is that these men were not professional or conscripted soldiers, but fiery, hot-headed volunteers who were so impatient to begin the greatest adventure of their lives that they set out at once in answer to England's call.

They went eagerly. Stout-hearted men such as Alexander Walder who left his bullock team standing in the middle of a paddock and walked twenty miles as soon as he heard about the arrival of a visiting Recruiting-Officer at Donald. They were men filled with a keen and dauntless spirit to fight against evil and fully prepared to die, if necessary, for the cause they believed in.

Did they not journey half-way across the world to fight brutal German hordes for the greatest cause of ail — "The Preservation of our Civilisation"?

Later, there was created amongst these men another fine quality of spirit known as "MATESHIP", yet how accurately can one define this uniquely-Australian attribute? Perhaps the closest definition is "Being able to trust your chum as much as he is able to rely on you". An Australian soldier would not give way to the enemy when he knew that his mates were depending upon him to stand firm and true — in fact, he would rather die than betray their trust and confidence.

The following letters reveal another admirable quality — a great love and filial respect towards their parents. They wrote home to "dear Mother and Father" in spite of distance, dangers and distractions; and although most of the soldiers left school at a very early age (even as young as eleven, or twelve) yet their letters are well-written. I have simply paragraphed them for easier reading.

Finally, I know we cannot possible understand the intense pain and suffering of those brave soldiers. Not even in our wildest imagination can we visualize the daily slaughter they experienced, although I think their letters can, and do, give us some inkling of the daily torment in their "LIVING HELL".

We know that when they began to evacuate the Turkish Peninsula the deepest regret of these troops was having to leave behind their dead mates. One soldier said, as he pointed towards a beach cemetery at Anzac Cove, "I hope they won't hear us marching down the gullies!"

Read this book and you will find a precious gift in the form of a "Living Memorial" from the ANZACS ————— and that is better than any cold, stone statue.

French soldiers

"DON'T GO--!"

was the advice of Mr. J. Wheeler, a Birchip farmer, to his drover, W. Lindsay, in December, 1914.

Dear Bill,

I did intend to have a lot to say about you going to the war. But thinking it over I have decided that it is none of my business. You have a right to please yourself about what you do. However, I do say think it over well before you take the final step. Remember that when you sign on, you are signing away your liberty and signing your own death warrant.

You will have worse hardships to face than you ever had working for me. You will be treated like a working bullock; you will be loaded up worse than a swagman and have a man over you all day roaring and swearing at you like a bullock-driver; and they don't care if you never get a feed. A thousand men rush up to a pot of stew like starving vultures and the last men get none.

Men in camp will wish they were back here, as it is marching and drudgery all day long on very little tucker. I have seen letters from the first lot to go saying they are having a rough time. Ten hours a day of solid marching and drill with a load on your back; and an officer roaring at you and only a hard biscuit and water for dinner — and no tea!

And after all this hardship what comes next? You are stood up to be shot at and the first bullet you stop is generally the last thing you will ever see. But then, who cares? You are just one of hundreds shot that day. And if you live through the bullets, and fever, and dysentery, and come back to Victoria, do the people make you Lord Mayor of Melbourne?

They didn't when I came back from the Boer War. They gave us a few free dinners and beers. Then after a few weeks they told us to go and get work. That was all the thanks we got, those of us who were lucky enough not to get shot. Enough said. You just think it over, son.

This veteran of the Great Boer War (1899-1902) gives a realistic picture of his army life — yet our drover did go, in spite of the farmer's predictions of hardship.

THE MOST DANGEROUS GERMAN RAIDER OF THE SEAS

The *Emden* was a small armoured German cruiser of 3,600 tons, with a speed of 25 knots and carrying ten 4 in. guns, eight 5-pounders, four machine-guns and two submerged torpedo tubes. She had a complement of 321 officers and men — and her commander, Captain Von Muller, soon became notorious for his craft and cunning. In fact, his ship became the most dangerous of all the German raiders that roamed anywhere and everywhere across the wide ocean.

It was September 10th. 1914, when this German raider attracted world attention by her daring actions. A British ship, the *Indus*, was lying in the Bay of Bengal when she was suddenly attacked by the *Emden* which fired a shot into her bows as it cunningly entered the Bay behind a collier. The *Indus* crewmen were taken prisoners by Captain Von Muller and then the *Indus* was sunk.

The next day the *Emden* sighted a British merchantman, the *Lovat*, and so proceeded to bomb and sink that unfortunate freighter. A few hours later another British ship, the *Kabinga*, was sunk — and later, that same day, a British trader, the *Killin*, was seized and also sunk by the *Emden*. Shortly after the *Killin* had been disposed of, another British merchantman, the *Diplomat*, was sighted and immediately sunk by the wily *Emden*.

Thus, within a couple of days, that German Raider had caused a great loss to the British economy — and still had not finished her cunning ways. On the evening of September 23rd. the *Emden* suddenly appeared near Madras harbour and started firing on the great oil tanks there, until four were set alight. But as soon as the Madras land forces began to fire back at the German raider, the *Emden* quickly slipped away. The damage done to those oil tanks was about 15,000 pounds. Soon, a great fleet of British cruisers was searching every corner of the seas in order to capture the dangerous *Emden*. Yet the raider's career was certainly not finished, for on the 20th. October she captured seven Indian merchant ships and sank five of them. The German cruiser's success was only made possible because the *Emden* was able to intercept wireless messages from the British, China and Indian stations.

On October 28th. the Russian cruiser, *Zhemtchug*, was quietly lying at anchor just outside Penang harbour when its crew noticed a strange vessel approaching which had four funnels and flying the Japanese flag. No-one recognised the notorious and dangerous German raider because everyone knew the *Emden* only had three funnels; but Captain Von Muller had cleverly disguised his ship by rigging up a dummy fourth funnel.

' *Emden* '
CAUGHT AT LAST

CAUGHT AT LAST

On Monday, November 9th. (1914), Australian and New Zealand troops from the decks of their transport ships had seen H.M.A.S. SYDNEY leave her place at their side. She steamed away in answer to an S.O.S message from the Cocos Islands, with thick, black smoke pouring from her four funnels. The message had said, "Strange warship approaching."

As H.M.A.S. SYDNEY steamed northwards, she sighted an enemy ship less than 60 miles away, and just over the horizon, from Australia's precious Convoy. As expected, it turned out to be the German cruiser, EMDEN. Here was, indeed, a bold adversary which had destroyed several British merchant ships within the past fewmonths.

It was 9-30 a.m. when H.M.A.S. SYDNEY sighted the EMDEN and began to close in on her. Then at 10-45 a.m. a wireless message arrived from the SYDNEY'S captain, saying, "Am briskly engaging enemy". Not long afterwards, at 11-10 a.m., came the signal, "EMDEN BEACHED AND DONE FOR".

THE END OF THE EMDEN

(From the diary of STOKER ELLIOTT *comes this exciting story. We read how a St. Arnaud man played his part in Australia's first, great naval battle of World War 1.)*

"I joined the Navy in 1912 and went to England on board H.M.S. DRAKE. I was a member of the crew to bring out the H.M.A.S. SYDNEY from Portsmouth to Australia in 1913. *(Three ships —* SYDNEY, AUSTRALIA *and* MELBOURNE *— arrived here in 1913 to form the beginnings of our Navy.)*

I was serving in the Northern Territory when word arrived that war had been declared. Thence we were ordered off to

German New Guinea on enemy patrol. Later, we had orders to proceed to Albany, in Western Australia.

With the H.MA.S. MELBOURNE and the Japanese cruiser, IBUKI, the SYDNEY had a responsible job of escorting our first Australian troopships to the war — 45 of them in number.

On the night of November 8th. we passed Cocos Island. The SYDNEY (being junior ship) was ordered by the MELBOURNE to proceed full speed to a reported trouble-spot. At the time we were 60 miles from the Island, but she gradually worked up full speed with 12 boilers and 36 oil sprayers. Our electric fans collapsed, and made it necessary to apply wet cloths to the mouths of the firemen. At 9 a.m. "Prepare for Action" was sounded.

WHILE THIS GREAT SEA-BATTLE RAGES THE OCEAN'S TOP IS TORN BY SHELLS.

Then a shell exploded and carried away our after-control (which controls the whole of the guns' fire) the control officer and four men being wounded. Captain Glossop then began manoeuvring the SYDNEY, which puzzled Von Muller, the captain of the EMDEN. Subsequently, her shots fell short

and the SYDNEY closed in. Now the EMDEN's shots were passing over us.

Captain Glossop's scheme answered well for a time, and then our tactics were altered. Throughout the battle, Captain

Glossop remained standing on the bridge. Soon we recognised the EMDEN's defeat. Her time was up.

At 10-5 a.m. the EMDEN's foremost funnel disappeared. At 10-20 a.m. our lyddite shells caused an awful explosion on the EMDEN, followed by a fire near the main masts, and nothing but a thick cloud of smoke was discernible.

Those on the SYDNEY at this period became overjoyed and so left their stations, but the EMDEN gave the SYDNEY another broadside and then every man flew back to his respective station. At 10-30 a.m. the EMDEN's foremast was completely shot away. At 10-40 a.m. her second funnel disappeared, followed by another loud explosion in the EMDEN's boiler-room. At 11-10 a.m. the third funnel and her bridge were shot away.

The crippled EMDEN now made for land, and at 11-15 a.m. she ran aground on Keiling Island. During this sea-battle, the EMDEN fired one torpedo (luckily passing our stern) and 1400 shells; whilst the SYDNEY fired one torpedo and 650 shells. The captured British collier was an observant onlooker throughout, and at the conclusion of the action made a bolt to escape from us. But our six-inch shell stopped her progress. Her colours were then demanded, but the German Ensign was destroyed by fire so it could not be secured by us.

An armed crew was sent aboard the collier to take charge, but our men were informed by the panic-stricken Chinese crew that the vessel had her sea cocks open and was filling rapidly. They begged to be rescued and taken aboard our ship. So their crew was brought aboard the SYDNEY and we then sank the collier by firing four shots into her.

The SYDNEY then made for the EMDEN and we saw the German Ensign still floating at the main mast. The

SYDNEY signalled three times, "Do you surrender?" but no notice was taken of our question. No reply being forthcoming, our gunners were ordered to fire at the foot of the EMDEN's main mast. But as the SYDNEY turned to fire her starboard guns, the EMDEN raised the white flag, and a sailor proceeded to haul down the German flag. The Germans again burnt their flag to prevent us capturing it. The EMDEN having surrendered, we then proceeded to rescue some of the EMDEN's crew who were badly burnt and had been in the water for several hours.

That night of the 9th. November, when the prisoners were being questioned, one of them reported that an armed party of 45 Germans had been put ashore on Cocos Island. As soon as daylight approached, the SYDNEY sent an armed party ashore, consisting of 45 officers and men; and when we neared the landing station, the islanders gave cheer after cheer, for they had been waiting our approach all night.

They informed us that the German party from the EMDEN, had captured a 70-ton island schooner early that very morning and made their escape. But had we landed sooner, on the night of 9th. November, the Germans had prepared a welcome for our party in the form of 4 mounted Maxim guns. We would have been wiped out! Thanks to the caution of Captain Glossop, our lives had been saved.

(OUR VICTORIOUS SAILORS SHOW RESPECT TO THE GERMAN WOUNDED.)
Captain Von Muller (true to naval tradition) was the last man to leave his ship. He surrendered his sword of office to our Captain Glossop; but later, he was handed back his sword and taken to Colombo as a prisoner.

On November 11th. we returned to our convoy and passed

through the lines of troopships whose soldiers lined the decks, cheering madly. But instructions were issued that no demonstrations were to be made, as we had wounded sailors on board. Later, they were transferred to the EMPRESS OF RUSSIA.

[133 Germans killed, with 65 wounded and 117 prisoners.]

(Stoker Elliott's *diary records many places he visited around the world. When in London, in 1915, he witnessed the first German Zeppelin brought to the ground. Yet, having seen the world, he writes that he has learnt one important lesson from it all —* "Australia is the best country in the world and I intend to remain in it.")

- H.M.A.S. "Australia", "Sydney", "Melbourne" — arrive in Australian waters from English shipyards in 1913

**WITH SMOKE POURING FROM HER FOUR FUN-
NELS, HMAS "SYDNEY" LEAVES HER PRECIOUS
CARGO TO CHASE THE "EMDEN".**

**MEN OF THE SYDNEY CHEERING AS THE EMDEN
RUNS ASHORE**

TRAINING IN EGYPT

Australian and New Zealand men of the First Convoy seat from here, landed in Egypt on December 7th. 1914 where they remained until the opening of the Dardanelles Campaign.

Their long months of training in the desert were terribly hard. It was TRAMP — TRAMP — TRAMP through the hot sands of the desert every morning; but the grueling exercise certainly made them fit for the fiery ordeal that lay before them on the Gallipoli Peninsula.

Unfortunately, some of their senior officers found desert conditions physically debilitating and injurious to their health. For example, Lieutenant-Colonel Semmens of the Sixth Battalion found that his health suffered in the extremes of this desert climate. Other senior officers were really too delicate for life at the Front and ended up being replaced by younger men.

The Australian 1st. Division was located at the picturesque setting of Mena Camp, about one mile from the three big Pyramids and the Sphinx. Although the days were hot, the men who had to sleep under the stars soon complained of rheumatics brought on by the very cold nights and heavy dews.

Many of the young men were tempted by the "Fleshpots of Cairo" — and soon venereal diseases became a big problem among the soldiers. It is sad to think that the military authorities did not educate their high-spirited soldiers about such dangers. These young men had never been away from home before and were "innocents abroad".

Private C. M. Alexander (of St. Arnaud) is in the Signal

Corps with the First Expeditionary Force in Egypt. He is writing from Alexandria.

<u>6th. December, 1914.</u>

DEAR MOTHER,

You will be Interested to learn that we have reached the above port after a long and not very eventful voyage. In which we called at Aden, Suez and Port Said; but as we were not allowed to land, we only had the pleasure of viewing these places from their harbours.

It would have given us all the greatest of pleasure to have seen more of Colombo. It looked a most interesting and inviting place with its handsome buildings and picturesque aspect. Looking through the telescope. I could see quite plainly, the people walking through the streets. They all wear the loose-fitting, coloured garments of their ancestors, unaffected by the change of fashions.

Aden, locked in by its barren heights, upholds its reputation as one of the most barren places on this earth. I don't think it will ever become a health resort! We left Aden after stopping there for twenty-four hours, then reached Suez and Port Said on Tuesday, after a voyage of seventeen hours.

I was surprised to see that the Suez Canal is not half so dreary a place as it is made out. Every hour we passed a village with brightly-coloured buildings and encampments of Indian soldiers (who are preparing to resist the Turks).

Port Said is a very interesting place. Its buildings are all brightly-painted and built in such quaint styles. The streets come right down to the water's edge, and are filled with strangely-attired inhabitants.

Over all, is the fascination and mystery of the East. After stopping at Port Said for a day, we passed on, gliding by a statue of De Lesseps, erected on the extremity of one of the breakwaters reaching out into the Mediterranean.

We are now at the scene of Lord Nelson's great victory, and are to proceed on to Cairo where Indian and Territorial troops are encamped. The Turks under Gamal Pasha are advancing on Egypt; but the enemy will get a warm reception when they reach the Canal.

I am on tiptoe with expectation to see the wonders of this ancient land. Alexandria extends along the shores of a crescent-shaped bay which is filled with the most curious vessels imaginable. CHARLES

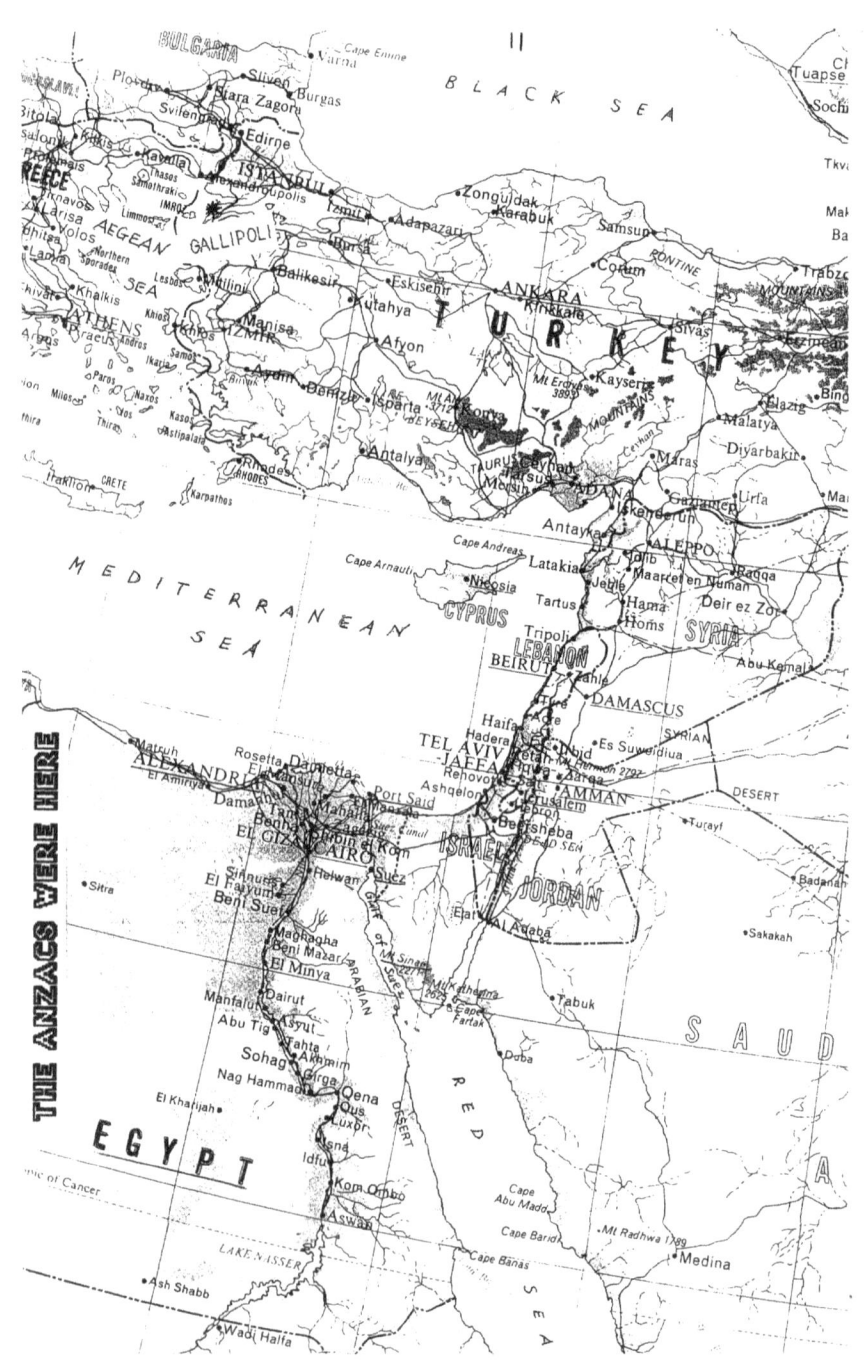

(ISTANBUL is the modern name for CONSTANTINOPLE)

ON BOARD THE TRANSPORTS

A BOXING COMPETITION
PHOTOS BY SERGEANT ALEXANDER WALDER

SMELLY CAIRO

Front Egypt, a *Birchip soldier* Private H. Wilson *A.I.F. writes in December,* 1914: -

I am satisfied that this particular part of Egypt we are camped in, is drier than the Mallee. It is a funny thing, though, that the second night we were here it rained for the first time for a very long while. We were underneath our oil sheets as it happened, or we would have got a trifle damp! Now we have seven tents to a company, and very few of us sleep outside.

I have had two journeys into Cairo already, and only been here in camp a week. There are some very good streets and some very bad ones. Around about old Cairo the streets are narrow and filthy; but in the modern part, the streets are wide and the buildings very modern.

We have got quite used to the Egyptian money now. and can talk 'piastres' by the yard. Their smallest coins are made of nickel, and are about the size of our sixpence (the present 5-cents coin). The 2. 5. 10. 20, 40, piastre coins are made of silver and get larger in size according to their value. The 40-piastre coin is about twice the size of our half-crown. We find we lose money when changing at small shops.

Well, for our trip. We all have to line up and be inspected by the guard when going on leave. We are marched in line to the tram-terminus before being dismissed. Then the poor old tram gets rushed by an excited mob. and the conductor gets nervous and agitated. So it takes longer to get on the tram than it should!

When in Cairo, our first place of inspection was a restaurant, and so we partook of a luxurious meal. I have not found a place yet where we can get fruit and cream; they don't seem to sell it. After the meal, we went off on a ramble with two English "terriers" (Royal Engineers), and they took us through the highways and byways of Cairo.

If you landed in Cairo from a balloon you would know the place by the smell. Every shop seems to have its quota of perfume. They are very poor shops in the lower quarters, but in the main streets there are some splendid shops. The streets are all curves and angles, and do not seem to bear any relation to our block system.

The second night we were in Cairo, we went skating. It cost 3 piastres for skates; and while you are whizzing around, moving—pictures are being shown, and it's A1. The first night we came back to camp in a horse-drawn cab as the trams were too crowded; but this kind of transport is too slow. So on the second night we motored back and did the journey in record time, passing everything else on the road.

Well. I've climbed the Pyramid. Our 'C' company had a tour on their own on Thursday morning, and then we had two hours to do as we pleased. We were dismissed at the Sphinx, and after a brief glance at this, we started to climb up the highest pyramid. We reached the top in about 15 minutes (471 feet) and climbing was fairly stiff in places. However, on the top we had a small cup of coffee and carved our names in the stone slabs. The space on top is only about 5 yards square, and you get a splendid view of Cairo which is 8 miles away — and of the surrounding district.

The Pyramid used to have a smooth face from top to bottom, of alabaster slabs; but that was in 3000 B.C. and since then the alabaster slabs have been taken down and used to build a palace for some Egyptian Prince in Cairo. Some of the slabs of stone, which make up the walls of the Pyramid, must weigh half-a-ton, and goodness knows how they got them up this height only using manpower (slaves).

Then we climbed down and hired a guide to show us through underneath. It's a weird place, if ever there was one! We entered a tunnel about 6 feet high by 3 feet wide, and went down a slope to the base of the Pyramid. Then up the slope — to what the guide called. "The King's Chamber", and we saw here a hollow tomb of some ancient Egyptian King. Then off this room is a small nook called the "sarcophagus" where Pharoah's daughters were embalmed. In two or three places our guide lit magnesium coils and they showed up the walls clearly, but made the shadows very weird.

It took us about half-an-hour to go through the rooms and when we came out we had our fortunes told, just for a joke, because they invariably tell everyone the same. I seem to be in for a good time, according to the teller. Dinner-time came and we were marched back to camp. Then, at 3 o'clock, we went on our second trip into Cairo, so we had an interesting day.

Now a few notes about the camp. On the first few days we were allowed to wander about and get our land-legs back (after being on the boat so long). Since then we have had a few route marches through parts of the desert, and a day at mixed battle tactics. A mile across the sand is equal to two on solid earth!

Alexandria Is full of German vessels that were seized at the declaration of war. They are mostly of small tonnage, and appear to be engaged in European (chiefly Mediterranean) trade only.

On the Sunday of our arrival at Alexandria, we had

orders to disembark on the following day (Monday). Reveille sounded at 5 a.m. and the 13th. Battalion disembarked at. 9 a.m. Orders then came through for the 14th.Battalion to stand by. So, at 2 p.m. the 14th. commenced a route march through Alexandria, returning to the ship at 4 p.m. We (the 15th. Battalion) were then ordered to disembark at 9 p.m. and to entrain at 9.30 p.m.

At 4.30 a.m. on the following Tuesday morning, tired and sleepy, we marched into Mena camp. We had a few hours' sleep, and then commenced fixing up the tents. Although it is six weeks since we arrived here, owing to all the strenuous training we have undergone, there are very few of us who have seen much more than Cairo and the Pyramids.

One of the most interesting places I have visited is about 4 miles from the camp. At this place, according to tradition, is the tree under which the Virgin Mary rested during her flight into Egypt (when she was escaping from the wicked King Herod). Also, I saw the well from which she quenched her thirst. The legend says that before Mary came to this well its water was brackish, but to quench her thirst its water miraculously became fresh. It is the custom to drink a glass of this water, and so we did, but it was no elixir by any means.

In the grounds containing the tree and the well, a church has been built. It is about the same size as the church at Surrey Hills. It is most magnificently-decorated inside. The altar is very beautiful and the walls are covered with paintings and small pieces of statuary, depicting incidents in the life of Jesus.

A few hundred yards further on from the temple is an obelisk. It is about 60 feet high, and is a solid block of granite. But compared with the Thames obelisk (at Westminster. London) I should think it is rather insignificant,"

THE TORPEDOING OF THE "LUSITANIA," MAY 7, 1915.
A reproduction of a picture postcard which was very popular in
Germany. The portrait is of Admiral von Tirpitz.

In Egypt

An unfortunate accident happed at Ismailia when one of our soldiers bought some oranges from an Arab lad, who ran away with-out giving any change out of half-a-crown. Of course the soldier was furious and gave chase on to a railway bridge over the canal, and not noticing a gap in the planks he fell into the water and was drowned."

Erecting Sheds

A Light Horseman

At Mena Camp.

Cairo Transport

Camped on the Sands

We are camped right behind the three Great Pyramids and the Sphinx. The pyramids are fascinating and are made of great stones, and I have been in one. You are allowed to climb these pyramids, but the other day a soldier was climbing one when he slipped and fell a long way to his death.

Signal Practice

Sight-seeing

Sergeant H. Young, of St. Arnaud, who left with the First Expeditionary Force, writes home from Egypt.

ANCIENT WONDERS
Mena Camp
December 10th. 1914

DEAR MOTHER, We arrived at Alexandria on Saturday, disembarked on Wednesday (Dec. 3rd.) and then left for Cairo.

The countryside from Alexandria to Cairo is the finest I have ever seen. Every acre is under cultivation; with cotton, date palms, Indian corn and rice being grown. The old wooden plough, drawn by a bullock, is still used; but the ground is tilled properly and would open the eyes of some of the Australian "cockies".

We arrived at Cairo about 8 p.m. and then went to Mena, about 10 miles distant from Cairo. We are camped right under the Pyramids, and on the old battlefield of Napoleon Bonaparte.

The Pyramids are wonderful. There are three of them. The highest is 480 feet, and the other two are about 400 feet. A party of us with a guide visited the third Pyramid, which is one of the most interesting. Inside, is the tomb of the Queen of Sheba and ancient Kings of Egypt.

The Sphinx is another wonderful piece of work. It is cut out of solid stone. Napoleon is said to have blown off the nose with a cannon ball. The temple of the Sphinx has pillars of solid granite. How they were placed there is a mystery to everyone. They were transported for ten miles.

An American syndicate is excavating for ancient treasures

around here at present. They are seeking the remains of the King of Mena. He was the third, or fourth, King of Egypt, and buried with him is a lot of the ancient history of Egypt — for which there is a big reward. The syndicate expects to be here digging for three months.

We are all anxious to get to the Front.

AN AUSTRALIAN TROOP-SHIP

kind regards to all at home.
Although I am so far from thee
And o'er the waters roam:
There's only one place dear to me
And that is "Home, Sweet Home."

COMMENTS ABOUT A
ARMY LIFE IN EGYPT

(Our soldiers were training on the edge of the Sahara desert) One chap wrote — "We are in Mena camp, about 10 miles distant from Cairo. We are camped right under the pyramids and on the old battlefield of Napoleon Bonaparte. We find lots of human skulls and large bones belonging to French soldiers who fought here long ago. The pyramids are wonderful. There are 3 of them. The highest is 480 feet high and we have been given permission to climb it.

The Sphinx is a wonderful piece of work cut out of solid stone. It is the statue of a couchant lion with the head of a Pharaoh wearing the royal head-dress and with a snake on the brow. Napoleon's soldiers were responsible for blowing off its nose with a canon ball."

(The Egyptian desert was a most unpleasant place for their camps) As one soldier wrote, "Yesterday was bad for dust. All day we could not see fifty yards ahead. The dust eats into one's eyes, grates on one's teeth and sticks ail over your clothes. At dinner we ate more sand than anything else. The only meat we get is camel.

The other day one of our soldiers bought some oranges and gave the lad 2/6 but the boy ran off without giving change. The soldier was angry and gave chase, but he did not see a gap between the planks of a wooden bridge and fell into the canal and was drowned."

"It is exciting to climb the pyramids and the view from the top is splendid," writes another, "but the other day a chap slipped and fell a long way down and died from his injuries.".

Many of those innocent young men were tempted by the FLESHPOTS OF CAIRO — AND SOON VENEREAL DISEASES BECAME A BIG PROBLEM AMONG OUR SOLDIERS. These young men had never been away from home before and were INNOCENTS ABROAD. It was not until 1917 that the military authorities warned soldiers about the "WOMAN PERIL".

TOM & BERT

CROCHETED QUILT MARY MADE FOR BERT.

A POSTCARD FROM EGYPT.

BERT MOYLE c 1916.

A Ship's Barber

*A Dhow on
the Nile*

Gurkhas

AN EGYPTIAN SHADOOF

An ancient Eastern invention for raising water. It consisted of a long pole working on a post and weighted at one end; whilst on the other end was attached a bucket that was lowered into the water and then raised when full.

CAIRO
a busy street

writing a letter home

Private Austin Davey often sent a picture card to his girl-friend Clem Pope, in Donald and his words on the back give us some idea of what it was like for soldiers training on the burning Egyptian sands in preparation for that assault on Gallipoli.

Dear Clem, It is amazing how many fellows I meet up with who were training with me at Broadmeadows. We have shifted again since I last wrote to you. I don't think it will be long now before we finally shift out of Egypt. The weather is still warm and the flies are very troublesome. I have taken to sleeping outside the tent now, but we won't have tents much longer. I have travelled quite a bit while over here just by shifting camp so often. I have not had a day's sickness and have been in every route march and have not fallen out of one — and by Jove we have had some stiff ones. Dozens of bigger fellows than me have had to fall out. I have got blisters on my feet now, but they will be all right in a couple of days. I suppose you have heard of the promotion of Major ------. He is a Lieutenant-Colonel now and wears a crown and a star. I am keeping tip-top and hope you are all well at home. From your loving Boy.

SUEZ - The Bazaar.

Lance-Corporal F. McRae Neal writes from Egypt:

"It is all Egyptian money (piastres) here and it is great fun trying to count it, but you soon get used to it. The Egyptian merchants try to beat us down for as much as they can when giving change, but we get even with them. They always ask about three times the price for an article. I bought a fountain pen from one native who could not speak a word of English, so it was a bit of fun making the deal. He wanted ten shillings at the start, but I beat him down and got it in the end for four shillings. I think we will be going to France (not Gallipoli) before long. The Indian soldiers can take care of the Turks and give them all the fighting they want. It won't be a hard job as there are enough of our men here to eat them. The Turks will wish they had died last winter before we are done with them."

(Unfortunately, it was not <u>easy</u> for the Anzacs against the well-entrenched Turks in Gallipoli — as we now know in hindsight.)

THE SANDS OF THE EGYPTIAN DESERT

"Yesterday was the limit for dust," writes a soldier from Egypt. "I never want to see the like again." From 6-30 a.m. till the evening we could not see fifty yards ahead. The dust eats into one's eyes, grates on one's teeth, and sticks all over the clothes. At dinner we ate as much of sand as anything else. It was rather hard luck to strike a day like this when we had about the best menu that it has yet been our fortune to have dished up before us — beef, pickles and vegetables. Some of the fellows brought their towels in to help them. They would take a mouthful and then cover their plates over lively to dodge the swirling sand. But oh, it put the 'acid' on that dinner."

POSTCARDS FROM EGYPT

THE CAMELEER AND HIS CAMEL

This humped, long-necked ruminant was made for desert life. In such regions the people depend on it for carrying them and their goods. Desert tribes rely on the camel, not just as a means of transport, but also as their only source of wool, milk and meat.

OBELISK OF HELIOPOLIS

This is a type of monument specially characteristic of ancient Egypt. It is a tapering shaft of solid stone, square in shape, with a pyramidal apex. It has hieroglyphics of the ancient Egyptian language upon its sides. The obelisk that stands upon the Embankment at Westminster, London, is nicknamed "Cleopatra's needle".

ASCENDING
THE GREAT PYRAMID

Notice how the man and woman need assistance from their native guides. The climb looks very difficult because of the huge, rough stones.

CAIRO — THE SPHINX

The Market, Ismailia   *Citadelle, cairo*

A GENERAL VIEW OF CAIRO

PYRAMIDS AND THE NILE DURING FLOOD

A VIEW OF THE PYRAMID OF CHEOPS

KASR — el NIL BRIDGE IN CAIRO

CAIRO — GENERAL VIEW OF THE CITADEL

CAIRO — BARRAGE BRIDGE

A NATIVE WOMAN

PYRAMIDS — BUFFALO ON THE NILE

RIVER NILE

PYRAMIDS AND THE NILE DURING FLOOD

CAIRO — MOHAMMED-ALY-MOSQUE

*A NATIVE
WOMAN*

*THE SULTAN
MASSAN
MOSQUE*

Private R. H. Barber (8th. Battalion) writes from Egypt to his friend, Mr. Gus. Beckham (of Jeffcott).

Mena Camp. <u>26th. December 1914.</u>

Dear Gus,

I hope you are all well at Pine Grove. Yesterday was Christmas Day — and we had a very fair day, considering our new surroundings and conditions. Our tent-mates had a good time. You see, about a fortnight before Christmas we collected money from each man in our tent to buy things for the 25th. December, which we called our "Grub Fund". Then, when we went out on leave, we purchased our <u>eatables</u>.

First, we caused great fun by asking for "a grocer's shop"- which was not an easy thing to find as every native we asked did not seem to "savvy". At last we met a chap who could speak English and he directed us to the right kind of shop. Arriving there, we asked for <u>Christmas puddings;</u> and, by the expression on the storekeeper's face, one would think we had asked for elephants, or fleas!

At last, with a lot of explanations and sign-language, we made him understand. We procured four puddings, four tins of pineapple, one tin of caramels, nuts, lollies, cake, four dozen oranges, and other sundries — these we buried in the sand inside our tent until Xmas Day (to save others the trouble of stealing them away!)

When the 25th. of December arrived we went to a church service, and, after being dismissed, we were allowed the rest of the day to ourselves. It was about 10-30 a.m. when we started to unearth our treasures; and then we took the puddings to a distant hill. Then we stole some wood and a kerosene tin and proceeded to cook those puddings. There were four of us engaged in this strenuous task; and after the puddings had been in the kerosene tin for only 10 minutes, one fellow reckoned they would be full of water and soggy if left any longer.

The rest of us replied. 'Yes, we supposed so," — seeing that we did not know anything about cooking puddings. On this knowledgeable chap's information we proceeded to examine them. Pulling one pudding out of its tin, we noticed it had risen a little — that seemed to be enough for us, for we could have sworn they were rising through the water getting into the tins.

We then proceeded to carry them back to the tent where the other chaps were eagerly waiting. But, by mistake, we left the puddings in the hot water in the kerosene tin and the consequence was they started to get sodden. Anyway, we had not boiled them for half the reasonable length of time — and you should have tasted those puddings. Well, bricks would have been soft in comparison to them. Anyhow, we laughed over our experiences — and had a good feed, considering the conditions.

Today (Boxing Day) we went for our usual tramp through the desert sands, and were glad to get back to camp. I have the honour of being elected "Battalion Scout", and every day I get a little extra work, separate from the others. Scouting is a risky game; but still, war is all chance. We are going out next week on "outpost duty" and will be out in the desert away from the camp all next week. This is far from pleasant work, but still it has got to be done as part of our training.

They have improved Mena Camp a lot lately by the making of reservoirs and roads; also, by putting up buildings — so I don't suppose we will be leaving here for a week or two, at least.

I climbed to the top of another pyramid yesterday, which was about 450 feet high, and on the top the natives were selling cups of coffee and food. You get a fine view from the top of the pyramid as you are up such a great height. Coming down is very hard, although not dangerous if you are careful; and, by the time you reach the bottom, your legs are shaking like leaves through the strain of descending.

There is an American excavating near the Pyramids, and he has been doing so for the last <u>ten</u> years. The natives here earn about six piastres a day (1/3d) — how would that wage suit the Australians? Our kind Colonel bought two oranges for each man in the 8th. Battalion as a kind of Xmas box.

We visited a Zoo near Cairo where every living wild animal imaginable is kept; but we did not have time to see the nearby museum with its collection of mummies.

We have jokes here about the various ways to spell pyramids (Perymids), Pharaoh (Fairo) and Cairo (Kiro). It keeps us amused.

MENA CAMP

The Beginning of Mena Camp in the Shadow of the Pyramids
(Xmas, 1914)

'The Ships of the Desert'

CAIRO

Corporal S. G. **Thomas** was formerly an employee of Mr. Samuel Coates of Donald. **Corporal "Gus" Thomas** sailed with the First Contingent of the "A.I.F."

Mena Camp,
CAIRO, Egypt.
January, 1915.

NOTHING BUT SAND
Dear Sam,
No doubt you will be surprised at getting a letter from me from this side of the world. But when you are away on these jobs with plenty of time to spare, you think of all your old friends; so I am writing to let you know that I haven't forgotten you.

Well, both Herb and I joined the First Australian Force to go and help to settle the difference between England and Germany. But we are dumped here in Cairo to finish our training, which is much better than being in England this time of the year.

We don't know when we will be shifted, or where we will be shifted to, but we have hopes of being in the big Spring army which will be going to the Front about March. In the meantime, we have a big chance of a "boxing match" with the Turks not many miles from here.

We left Melbourne on October 18th. on the good ship HORORATA. We waited at Albany for a week to get the fleet together, and then made tracks for Colombo (Ceylon). I doubt if there was ever a finer sight than that of our fleet as it was moving off.

We had 28 Australian troopships and 10 New Zealand transports — with 9 warships as our escorts. It looked real well. We had a very calm trip all the way, with nothing of much interest, except of course our encounter with the EMDEN, which the SYDNEY completely settled — but of course you will have read all about that, so I needn't explain it!

We had a 14 days' run to Colombo, but we never actually landed, so I can't tell you anything about it. But the place looked very well from the harbour.

Our next stop was Aden, which so far as we could see is purely a garrison port. We then went on to Suez. The weather was terribly hot, and the water was still and calm as a mill pond. The most interesting part of the trip was through the Suez Canal — which took us 16 hours.

The Canal has strong fortifications all along the banks on either side and they are manned by a very strong force. There is a bit of talk that some of our troops may be sent there also, but I hope it is not my luck to be picked for that job! This is bad enough, but that would be worse. At least we have a good city to visit when we are on leave, but there it would be nothing but the camp — and desert sands.

We landed at Alexandria after exactly seven hours from Suez, and went by train to Cairo (which is about 130 miles inland). We passed through some of the finest country in the world. Every inch of the way from Alexandria to nine miles past Cairo is irrigated from the River Nile.

The countryside is a network of channels, and the crops of maize and lucerne which are growing at present would open your eyes. But the real old-style of fanning is still here — an old wooden plough drawn by two oxen. It is the only farm-implement that I have seen.

The camel does most of the heavy carting, of course, on its back; and a farm doesn't seem complete without a dozen donkeys. I am told the land is worth 200 pounds an acre.

We are camped on the edge of the Sahara Desert, just at the foot of the Pyramids, and talk about SAND! It's a mass of loose sand for miles all around our camp — as far as I have been. I can only see SAND!

This sand is what we have to do our training on, so you can guess what the work is like. I sometimes wish that I had been born a CAMEL. But we are getting used to it now and I daresay we will have worse things to complain about when we get into the firing-line (fighting our way through Germany).

But taking this show all round, we are having a good time. I have got one stripe out of the Job so far and I hope it won't be long before I get two! It would mean a rise of 4 shillings a day, or 10 shillings in all — so it is worth trying for. I am sending a card with the picture of the Sphinx with the Pyramids in the background.

We are camped half-a-mile away. I am sending my address on the back of this, so don't forget to write — it will be nice to hear some news from Donald. Remember me to all old friends, GUS."

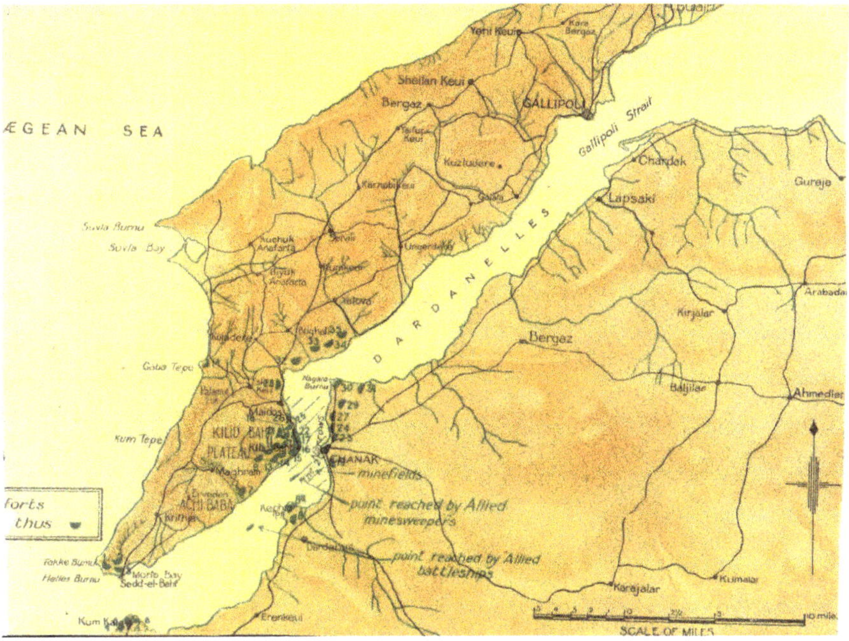

En Route to Gallipoli

Towed ashore in little boats

*Barbed wire on jagged metal poles laid
by the Turks all along the cliff tops*

Transport Ships

Digging In

THE LANDING ON ANZAC BEACH

Sentry Duty

On Lemnos Island

Anzac Cove

THE LANDING AT GALLIPOLI

It was in 1914 that thousands of young Australian men left the security of their homes and went off to war. They went eagerly, swept along by Andrew Fisher's patriotic words, "We shall stand by the Motherland to defend and protect her to our last man and our last shilling."

Throughout the fighting, Generals kept throwing their men against barricades of barbed wire and barrages of machine-gun fire; but it was the suicidal attack on The Nek (Gallipoli) that was one of the bloodiest and most appalling losses faced by our soldiers in that First World War.

Each year, on April 25th, Australians commemorate the Gallipoli Landing when over 90,000 allied troops, most of them British and Australian, stormed ashore upon the Turkish Peninsula to meet stiff resistance from enemy forces. It was unfortunate that the original plan to send Royal Navy ships and penetrate the main Turkish defences, stationed along the Narrows, was such a failure.

A Donald man, Richard Milbum, was a sailor in the Grand Fleet when his ship was sent to bombard those Turkish forts in February, 1915, and he describes the experience in a letter to his brother, Joseph Milbum.

"While our ship was firing, we were rather too close for comfort and several shots from the forts came very close to us. During those three weeks in the Dardanelles our casualties on board were 30 killed and 170 wounded. I would like to have known the Turkish losses. After taking our wounded sailors back to Malta we returned to the Dardanelles and were there when two of our ships, OCEAN and

IRRESISTIBLE, were sunk; but we were lucky as there were about 750 sailors on each of those two British ships, yet we only lost 7 men.

However, when the French ship, BOUVET, was sunk, the French lost about 560 men out of a crew of 800. But we eventually had to withdraw because more of our ships were lost to the many floating mines that protected Turkey's narrow stretch of water."

Unfortunately, this failed naval attack warned the Turks of their danger and gave them time to prepare powerful beach defences against any military force that might attempt to land on their Peninsula.

Thus, when the noble 3rd. Brigade landed at 4-30 a.m. on Sunday, April 25th. they faced a well-prepared and well-entrenched enemy who were both expecting and waiting for them.

Several Donald district soldiers took part in the landing on Ari Burnu beach — and in these following extracts from their letters we can imagine that terrifying experience.

Lt. Charles Barrie (8th. Btn.) "It was their baptism of fire as probably no troops had ever received before. Yet they fought like veterans and when ordered to advance there was no stopping them. There was never a word of complaint from the wounded, though it was terrible to see the poor chaps falling down all around me."

Pte. C. G. O'Brien (5th. Btn.) "It was while I was kneeling rifle in hand that I got wounded in the leg. I called out for help and Keith replied, 'I'm coming'. Then I heard a thud and saw Keith fall down, shot through the heart. I crawled back to

Neale and found him dead, too. The enemy sniper who killed both my mates was only a few yards away."

<u>Pte. J.M. Wemyss</u> (5th. Btn.) "We had a tough job as we landed in the face of heavy artillery and rifle and machine-gun fire and climbed the side of a steep hill that was rough and scrubby like monkey nuts. We could not see the enemy, although the Turks could see us. They played their machine-guns and shrapnel upon us with deadly results."

<u>Gunner Alfred Power</u> (6th. Btn.) "When we landed, boats filled with dead were lying all along the beach and the air was alive with bursting shells and flying bullets. We hastily buried 50 men in one grave; they belonged to the 7th. Battalion, poor chaps."

<u>Pte. J. Greenwood</u> (5th. Btn) "My rifle was smashed by a piece of shrapnel so I had to replace it with a dead man's gun. On the beach the sights were awful. There were bodies of our chaps floating all around and the dead and dying were scattered along the shoreline."

<u>Pte. A Forrester</u> (6th. Btn.) "I consider myself lucky as quite a number of my 6th. Battalion were killed and wounded as we were going ashore in the small boats. Two boats near me were blown to pieces with the men in them and each boat carries 30 men. Somehow I worked my way up to the front line across the bullet-swept hills. The enemy was throwing shells in threes and fours all day. The shells that hit men took half their body and their heads clean off. I saw some awful sights."

Pte. J. Hoare (14th. Btn.) "It took about three hours to get us to the Gallipoli Peninsula from Mudros habour. That Sunday saw our first taste of fire, but the boys stuck to it like glue and after a solid scrap we took a piece of land. We gave the Turks a good belting. They had a big shake-up, but I cannot tell you how many men we lost in the fighting."

A returned veteran once wrote, "It is only politicians who have neither fired a shot, nor heard the shrieks of the wounded, who cry aloud for more blood and more vengeance."

AUSTRALIA'S GREATEST BATTLE

Gallipoli Landing — Sunday, 25ᵗʰ. April, 1915.

Their success will go down in history when on that first Sunday 16,000 Anzacs managed to land by boat at Gallipoli, where, against the odds, three Australian brigades climbed tier after tier of cliffs beneath heavy Turkish fire and managed to reach the heights above the beach.

Landing at the Dardanelles

"The sight of the dead and wounded, absolutely covering the little sandy beach which runs along the mountain's base and just about 100 feet wide, was terrible — some already dead and tipped off the stretchers into heaps as they were brought down from the hills, whilst others were slowly dying for want of attention, with their life-blood oozing away."

A SHIP OF THE ROYAL NAVY
(Friend of the Anzacs)

AUSTRALIANS AT THE DARDANELLES.

GREAT GALLANTRY SHOWN.
TROOPS LANDED IN DARKNESS.
HEROIC DEEDS.
(Sunday, 25th, April, 1915.)

The following graphic account of the Australian troops' first encounter with the Turks was written by a British war correspondent, Mr. A. Bartlett of the "Daily Chronicle", who was on board one of the destroyers. The Australian Prime Minister, Mr. Fisher, authorised copies of it to be sent to all State Schools so that Head-Teachers could read it to their pupils.

The landing of the Australians at Gaba Tepe required splendid skill, organisation and leadership to get the large Armada under way from Mudros Bay (Lemnos island).

The warships and transports were divided into four divisions. Never before had the attempt been made to land so large a force in the face of a well-prepared enemy.

At 2 o'clock on the 24th. April, the flag-ship of the division of Australians passed the long line of slowly-moving transports amid tremendous cheering. They were played out of the Bay by the bands of the French warships.

At 4 o'clock the ships combined and troops assembled on deck to hear the Admiral's proclamation to the combined forces. This was followed by the last service before battle, the chaplains praying for victory.

At 1 o'clock on the next morning they reached their

rendezvous, five miles from the landing-place. The Australians who were about to go into action for the first time (under very trying circumstances) were cheerful, quiet and confident.

As the moon waned, the small boats were swung out from their pivots. Each boat was in charge of a young midshipman. They were loaded with great rapidity in absolute silence and without a hitch. Then the boats were towed ashore by six steam-pinnaces.

At 4 o'clock three battleships (a-line and four cables apart) arrived 2,500 yards from the shore. Their guns were manned and their searchlights got ready for action.

Very slowly the boats (filled with troops) were towed towards the shore. The battleships followed until the water shallowed. Every eye was fixed upon those hills, menacing in the gloom, whose mystery those men in the boats were about to solve.

The progress of the boats was slow. Dawn rapidly broke, and at 4-50 a.m. the enemy showed a light which flashed for ten minutes and then disappeared. The little boats appeared, almost as one, upon the beach. Seven destroyers glided noiselessly towards the shore at 4-57 a.m.

A sudden, sharp burst of rifle-fire from the boats relieved the prolonged suspense which had become almost intolerable. The firing lasted for a few minutes, then a faint British cheer floated across the still water, telling that the first position had been won.

The following boats had almost reached the beach when a party of Turks, entrenched ashore, opened a terrible fusillade from rifles and machine-guns. Fortunately, most of their bullets went high. The Australians did not wait for orders or for the boats to reach the beach.

They sprang out into the sea, formed a sort of rough line, and rushed the enemy's trenches. The magazines of their rifles were not charged, so they went in with the cold steel. It was all over in a minute. All the Turks in the first trench were either bayoneted or had run away.

The enemy held the second trench to the North strongly, and poured down a terrible fire upon the troops below and upon the boats pulling back to the destroyers.

The Australians stopped for a few minutes to pull themselves together, got rid of their packs, and charged their magazines. Then, this race of athletes proceeded to scale the cliffs without responding to the enemy's fire.

They lost some men, but in less than half-an-hour they had the Turks flushed out of their second position, the enemy either being bayoneted or flying.

The country, in which the landing was effected, is ideal for snipers — as the Australians soon found to their cost. On the other hand, the Australians also proved themselves adept at this kind of warfare.

In the early part of the day, the Australians suffered heavy casualties in the boats which conveyed the troops from the destroyers, tugs and transports. Yet this work of disembarkation proceeded mechanically under a point-blank fire. The moment each boat touched the beach, the troops jumped out and rushed for cover from that merciless hail of bullets. But the gallant boat-crews (often mere sailor boys of 16 or 17) had to pull in and out many times under that galling fire.

The disembarkation afterwards proceeded uninterruptedly, except for incessant sniping. But these Australians, whose blood was up, instead of entrenching, rushed north and east, searching for fresh enemies to bayonet.

The fact that it was difficult country in which to entrench

made the Australians prefer to advance further inland. Some men, who had pushed on too far, were counter-attacked and almost out-flanked by on-coming Turkish reserves, and so had to fall back after suffering heavy losses.

The Turks continued to counter-attack the whole afternoon, but the Australians did not yield a scrap of ground. Most of their troops were concentrated in a very small area; and, unable to reply, they were exposed to a relentless, unceasing shrapnel fire. Fortunately, most of it was badly-aimed. Both sides worked incessantly day and night.

The courage displayed by the wounded Australians will never be forgotten. In spite of their suffering, as they lay on the beach, they cheered the ships from which they had set out that very morning. These wounded soldiers were happy because they had now been tried for the first time — and had not been found wanting!

For 15 mortal hours the Australians had occupied heights under incessant shell-fire, without the moral or material support of a single gun ashore. They were subjected the whole time to violent counter-attacks from a brave enemy, skilfully-led, and with snipers deliberately picking off every officer.

There has been no finer feat in the history of this war than the Australians' sudden landing in the darkness and their storming of the heights; and, above all, holding on while reinforcements were landed.

These raw Colonial troops in that desperate hour proved themselves worthy to fight side by side with the heroes of Mons, the Aisne, Ypres and Neuve Chapelle.

Early on the morning of the 26th, April, the Turks repeatedly tried to drive the Australians from their position. But the Australians made a counter-attack and drove off the enemy with their bayonets, which the Turks would never face.

Although the Turks had been greatly-reinforced overnight, the Colonials made their sudden charge, with flash of bayonets, before which the Turks broke and fled. The enemy fell back, sullen and checked.

The Turks kept up an incessant fire throughout that second day; but the Colonials were now dug in and nothing could move them. Some Turkish prisoners, including their officers, stated that the Turks were becoming demoralised by the British Naval gunfire, and that the German commanders were having great difficulty in getting the Turks to attack.

WAITING AT MUDROS BAY — ON APRIL 24th.

THE LANDING ON APRIL 25th. 1915.

A TRIBUTE TO OUR
NOBLE THIRD BRIGADE

On that fateful day — Sunday, April 25th. — it was the officers and men of the 3rd. Brigade who bravely led the way up those steep, scrub- covered, inhospitable slopes of the Gallipoli coast.

That day was also the beginning of a long, drawn-out struggle for mastery of the Turkish Peninsula which was to end in a disappointing disaster for the British and the French.

At the beginning of the war Britain was really concentrating all her efforts in France, until Winston Churchill had this brilliant plan to capture the Dardenelles and thus join forces with Russia to isolate Turkey.

Consequently, in March, 1915, Royal Navy ships were sent to destroy the Turkish forts stationed along the Narrows; but these ships soon had to withdraw after losing several of their number to floating mines. Unfortunately, this failed naval attack warned the Turks of their danger and gave them time to prepare powerful beach defences against any military force that might attempt to land on their shores.

No wonder when Ian Hamilton arrived on 25th. April with his troops the Turks were there, waiting with a superior force to greet them; and so the poor Australians and New Zealanders were given the seemingly impossible task of landing on beaches beneath a deadly hail of bullets.

Let no one deny that the Turks have fine fighting qualities and that they suffered the same bloody slaughter as our own soldiers, yet there is no finer feat in the history of war than the storming of Gallipoli Heights by Australian volunteers.

When the noble 3rd. Brigade landed at 4-30 a.m. they faced a well-prepared and well-entrenched enemy who was both expecting and waiting for them. On that day the noble 3rd. Brigade lost 1,803 men — killed, wounded, or missing.

Can you imagine it? Those small, open boats, under a hail of bullets from the Turks' hidden guns, pouring out their men in thousands upon the beach below steep, rocky cliffs.

Climbing those heights looked to be a sheer impossibility. But they did and when one soldier heard the words to retreat, he said, "No way, I've only just got here."

Indeed, it was a deed whose gallantry has never been out-shone.

And WHO were these soldiers who did it? It was not the achievement of professional soldiers. NO. These were men from sheep-stations — from the Australian bush — or from the fields and townships of Australia and New Zealand, who, only a few short months before, had no idea of war and its challenges.

But when the call came, they responded they were volunteers and keen to begin the greatest adventure of their lives.

As one observer said after the battle, "I have never before seen men like those wounded Australians. They were happy because they had been tried for the first time and had not been found wanting."

And a young New Zealand soldier wrote in a letter home,

"The Australians were magnificent and deserve every good word that is said of them."

Did you know that more than 400 Aboriginal men fought in the First World War?

THE LANDING

Private C.G. O'Brien (5th. Battalion) was wounded at the landing on Gallipoli. He describes what happened in this letter to his parents.

Dear Mother,

We landed at 9 a.m. on 25th. April. For about 500 yards from the beach it was HELL, The Turks' shooting was excellent, especially their artillery which had all necessary ranges marked to a nicety, and their shrapnel was deadly. We were fighting all that day.

At 4 in the afternoon, our firing-line was being harassed by snipers and so the officer-in-charge called for a party to fix bayonets and scour some of the scrub in front of us. About 30 of us went out, but the snipers evidently saw us coming and retreated. We could not find anyone there.

However, we got down in the scrub and kept a good look

around. I found myself unexpectedly beside two of my tent-mates, Keith McIlwraith and Stan Neale. Suddenly word was passed around that we were being enfiladed on the left.

I jumped up and saw a Turk 50 yards away against the sky-line. I was just going to fire when the thought struck me that he might be an Indian as we had been especially warned, only the night before, not to mistake them and treat them as Turks. Others shared the same opinion that he could be an Indian.

It was all thick scrub and pretty high so you could not possibly see five yards in front of you. Well, the three of us stayed looking out for the enemy; while in the meantime, although we did not know it, the rest of our Company had retreated.

After a short time, as I was kneeling rifle in hand, I got my little dose. Neale came to my assistance, took off my heavy equipment, tore my trousers free from the wound and took out my field-dressing from my pocket. He called out to Keith McIlwraith (who was a little distance away) to come and help as I was hurt.

Keith replied, "I'm not going away," and immediately afterwards I heard a thud and Keith fell dead, shot through the heart by a sniper. Neale was distracted at losing his life-long friend and went straight to him, but could do nothing for him. I thought my leg was broken but found it was not when I struggled to get up. I scrambled up to go to Keith and found him sure dead.

As the enemy was only a few yards away, I crawled off and lay on my stomach for a breather. But then a bullet ploughed itself into the earth right beside me. I jumped up and cleared a bush, tearing myself amongst the brambles, with the bullets whistling around me as thick as bees in a hive.

I came to a ravine which was between our firing-line and

the Turks. On the brink of it, my right knee gave way and I fell down there, the bushes breaking my fall. I managed to slide forward on my back, thus protecting my leg. I got up and looked across at our firing-line and saw a few levelling their rifles at me.

I waved my hand and then dashed across the ravine, still exposed to the enemy's fire. As my leg was bleeding profusely and I was feeling somewhat weak and faint, I dropped down beside a dead man and took his field-dressing and tried to stop the flow of blood; but without success, and the bullets seemed uncomfortably close.

Then I made a dash for our firing-line — which I all but reached when I could go no further. A brave chap ran out and dragged me behind a bush where he dressed my wound as best he could. A few moments afterwards a chap in our Company named Anderson, came out to see who it was. They both started to carry me to the stretcher-bearers. Very shortly after this our whole line retreated, so I was just in time.

I was carried down to the beach about half-past ten at night, having to be pushed up steep sides of valleys and through thick scrub. At last I was put down in an open pontoon on my back, with my coat off and thrown across my leg. We left the beach at 5 next morning.

In the meantime it rained on and off and I was saturated; and all the time the Turks were firing on us, but only hitting the sides of the boat. I think they must have been firing blindly. Anyway, we got to the "Homes" about 6 on Monday morning, and left for Alexandria next day at 4 in the afternoon.

There was not enough accommodation on the hospital ship and for two days I had to lie on the open deck; until finally they got me into one of the very few cabins by turning out some poor chap who was less seriously wounded.

The first night I had two doses of morphia and one opium sleeping-drought, but even that couldn't send me to sleep. I lay awake all night long, listening to the battle raging without ceasing all that night and all the next day and night — right up till the time our ship left (about 2-30 p.m. on Tuesday, 27th. April). The fighting never stopped, not for one minute.

How much longer it lasted, I don't know, but the Navy had joined in by this time and were giving it to them strong. My hospital ship arrived at Alexandria at about 8 p.m. on Thursday, 29th. April. That night they only took off the few who could walk. I was taken off the following afternoon and brought here.

Strange to say, this is a German hospital. The nurses are all German, and there is a German doctor with some English doctors assisting him. They say they did not send these people away because they were so good; and they are certainly very good to us. We could not be treated better anywhere else, and it is a beautiful hospital, too. We all consider ourselves very lucky to be here.

Some of our fellows were sent off to England a few days ago to make more room. They only send those who would not be fit for duty for at least six weeks, yet who can get about and manage for themselves on the ship. The doctor had a look at me, but decided I would have to remain here till I mended up a bit He said he might send me later on when I am able to get out of bed.

I hope I can go, as I would love to see England, and I could get better just as well there as here. Well, mother, I'm afraid I must stop. I will write again, and in the meantime I can assure you I am doing very well. Why, when the nurse sits me up to make my bed, I can sit there myself without support for a couple of minutes now. I could not do that a few days ago, so you see I am on the mend.

Just now, I was taken away to have my wound dressed, and the doctor says I am to have my leg X-Rayed again and then they will see about extracting the bullets. So I am going to get them out after all. It appears there was some mistake about them — they thought I had rifle bullets, and when I told them they were shrapnel pieces, they said the bullets would have to come out as being leaden balls they are too dangerous. So that will mean a little operation today, or tomorrow. But it will be mild.

The doctor has just asked me if I would like to go to England. There is another ship-load going. You can guess my answer. I don't know when we leave.

Tell Syd. that Captain Hodgson who used to be in the old Scottish and was with us, is killed; he would know him.

I did not tell you, but I had great luck, in a way, as I would certainly have been killed except for the fact that Captain Sergeant was sitting next to me and he got half the charge. It killed him. poor chap, and had he not been beside me, I would most certainly have got it. I was terribly sorry as he was one of the best in the world.

Goodbye, mother, and give my love to all. CHARLES.

[Historian C.E.W. Bean writes — "When the first half of the 8th. Battalion arrived at Bolton's Ridge, it saw men far ahead upon Pine Ridge. Lieutenant-Colonel Gartside (second-in-command of the 8th.) ordered the leading companies forward. Major Sergeant was killed and Lieutenant Barrie wounded by the same shell, just as they were starting to advance,"]

KILLED DURING THE LANDING ON 25TH. APRIL, 1915.

Pte. C.S. Polkinghorne

Pte. Arthur Forrester.
Survived Gallipoli.
Killed in France,
1917

THE ARTILLERY-MEN ARRIVE AT ANZAC COVE

Anzacs unload a battery of Howitzers at Gaba Tepe, a few days after the storming of Anzac Cove. While the guns are being unloaded, these men are targets for the unseen foe who are firing down upon them. The enemy's guns are safely hidden behind the many rocky ridges along this coastline.

THE TRENCHES IN GALLIPOLI

(Photo: Gunner Geddie Fraser)

SERGEANT J. REYNOLDS, *back from the war, relates his experiences to a welcoming crowd in St. Arnaud.*

"We had been training on the sands of Egypt for some time, so we were all delighted when we received orders to go to the front. We sailed to Lemnos Island and stayed there for two weeks, having to undergo a daily routine of practising disembarkation whilst carrying full equipment on our backs.

When we were ordered to sail to Gallipoli, there was great jubilation and there was not a down-hearted man amongst us. As we neared the coast, our huge transport ships stopped about three or four miles off shore and so we had to be transported the rest of the way in small rowing boats known as 'pinnaces'.

When we stepped onto the beach between 3 and 5 o'clock in the morning of the 25th. of April the fun began. Every man had been given instructions to make the best of it as soon as he landed. Whilst our British warships were bombarding the heights, Turkish forts along the cliffs were firing down upon the beach where our soldiers were landing.

The guns of Gaba Tepe were eventually silenced by the big British warships, but we found the country was very difficult to cross as the hills rose to heights of 300 feet, or more. But we managed to chased the Turks inland and then entrenched.

Australians did splendid work, as did the English Tommies and the French and Indian troops. In the trenches every man's dug-out was his palace — and when a soldier in the firing-line was wounded, he was bandaged by a comrade and removed as quickly as possible to a hospital on the beach, where he was quite safe. There was great danger, however, when being rowed to board the transports as shrapnel was flying about everywhere.

Two days after landing I was badly wounded. I was shot through the right arm and the sinews were shattered, so now I carry my arm in a sling. A second bullet struck my lower jaw and the broken bones in my face had to be removed by the doctors in hospital, thus causing a facial disfigurement. In hospital we received the best of attention and every possible comfort. Wounded soldiers fully appreciate and are very thankful for the gifts of wearing apparel and comforts sent to them from the people of Australia. Remember, the Australian soldier is the best paid in the world — also remember he is a VOLUNTEER soldier!"

LANCE-CORPORAL BRODRIBB, *of St. Arnaud, enlisted in Western Australia and returned recently with other soldiers from Gallipoli. He describes how he was wounded in 1915.*

"When volunteers were called for, a party of 100 men came forward. We had orders to accompany Captain Leane and Lieutenant Rockliffe and endeavour to take possession of the observation station on Gaba Tepe from which the Turks were directing the fire of their guns down onto the transports, battleships and landing parties. The miners from the goldfields of Western Australia readily responded until our attacking party consisted wholly of soldiers from Kalgoorlie and Boulder.

British warships had shelled the hill night and day, but the Turks crept back under cover of night and continued to hold it. Just before daybreak we set out from the beach in open boats drawn by a pinnace and led by a torpedo boat, to the foot of the cliffs some two miles south of where we landed. The torpedo boat took us in as close as was possible and then we were cast off and had to row our three boats towards the shore until they grounded.

We then ran to within about 200 yards of the foot of the hill, but a terrible fusillade of fire opened on us from concealed machine-guns and wounded many of us. It was just like the original landing of April 25th. over again.

We fixed bayonets and scaled the heights in no time, but as soon as we poked our noses over the top of the cliff we found that the ground we had to cross was just a mass of wire entanglements and from our point of view it was impregnable. Then a signal came from the torpedo boats telling us to retire and this was apparently the only thing we could do. However, by now we had a lot of wounded to care for and these men could not be left behind.

On looking around for stretcher bearers it was discovered that of the four who had accompanied us three had been killed and one was seriously wounded. So volunteers were called for to stay behind and bring back the wounded — and I was one who offered.

I made three trips down the hill carrying stretcher cases, and was just about ready to leave with the last boat when I saw a private of 'A' Company lying on the ground. I called out, "What's the trouble, Joe?" He replied that he had stopped a bullet in his leg and was helpless because he could not walk.

I threw him over my shoulder and on getting to the beach found that the last boat had drifted some 300 yards out to sea, so I had no alternative but to wade into the water after it. All the time machine-guns were firing down on us and bullets flew around wildly. The waves were up to my chest by the time I reached the boat, so a wounded man leaned over the edge to assist me and my comrade.

Suddenly, the Turks appeared to get our range and the lead fell thick around us. The man in the boat was shot dead and so was the comrade on my back. So the man I was helping saved me from being struck on the head — the only part of my body that was exposed was my arms and I got three bullets in the left and two in the right, causing compound fractures of the right arm and a smashed left hand.

Although bullets hit me under water, the buoyancy of the sea saved me many serious wounds. I climbed into the boat somehow and eventually found myself being attended to by a doctor. It was certainly hot while it lasted.

I spent nineteen months during the South African War (1899-1902) fighting Boers, but the experiences of that campaign were a picnic compared to the present business."

THE NOBLE 3RD. BRIGADE

*Private **Arthur E. Forrester**, (6th. Battalion.) of Curyo, writes to his mother from Egypt, describing the Landing at Gallipoli on Sunday, 25th. April, 1915.*

Base Hospital,
Heliopolis Palace Hotel.
5th. May, 1915,

DEAR MOTHER,

I would have written a week ago, but could not find any writing-paper. I managed to get down to the main gate last night, and asked one of the boys to buy me some up the street. I suppose you know that I have been hit in the arm with a bullet. I daresay they will have sent home a casualty-list. I got a bullet in my right arm, and it is still in there; it is rather awkward for writing. It must be pressing on the nerves of my little finger and the one next to it, as they have been quite numb ever since I got the bullet.

They are going to X-Ray my arm today and take the bullet out; it has been in since 25th. April. It proves that nickel bullets, as used today, are not harmful as far as blood-poisoning is concerned. Only for it stopping the use of my two fingers, it could stay in altogether.

It seems unfair that after doing 8 months' hard training, I only last 8 hours on the battlefield. Better luck next time! Then, again, I can consider myself lucky, as quite a number of my 6th. Battalion were killed and wounded as they were going ashore in the boats. A couple of boats near me were blown into pieces, with the men in them. (Boats usually carried about 30 men).

We landed on the Peninsula side and It was a terrible landing. I will never forget it. We had the big naval guns to help us, and they had silenced all the Turkish guns, except one which was situated in the fort overlooking the bay. This was the one that was doing a lot of damage to us as we went ashore. After about an hour-and-a-half, with the help of a sea-plane, they got its position and finished the gun off.

I would say, if anyone asked me, that we landed under great difficulties. One shell landed just behind our boat; it was a narrow shave I can assure you, but that was only <u>one</u> of the dozens of narrow escapes we had on that Sunday.

The Turks had a lovely position on top of a high hill, right overlooking the beach; and as we were getting out of the landing-boats they opened fire on us with their rifles. They can't shoot for sour apples; if they could shoot straight, not a man of us would have been able to land.

<u>The 3rd. Brigade</u> were the first to land, and the only thing they could do (while the Turks were up above them) was to fix bayonets and charge up the slopes, and you should have seen the cowardly Turks run — they ran for their lives! A few snipers that were well-concealed, picked off many of our men, until they themselves were discovered, and then they would throw up their hands and cry, "Mercy, English." They got no mercy, but they got half-a-dozen rifles fired at them instead.

We were ordered to follow the Turks as they retreated. This was quite early in the morning of <u>Sunday, 25th. April.</u>

I did not tell you about the journey. After we left Mena Camp we entrained for Alexandria and there boarded the ship, S.S. GALEKA. We sailed as far as the Greek island of Lemnos. We stayed there about a week, waiting for the whole of our troops to arrive. There were about 110 boatloads of us when we moved from there, escorted by a number of warships.

We left early on <u>April 25th</u> so as to get to our landing-place while it was still dark. They hoped to take the enemy by surprise — but the Turks found out and were waiting for us. As soon as It was daybreak, the battleships began to speak — shells were bursting around our boats and you could hear the crackle of the rifles on the shore. It was only then, I think, that we realised what we were about to take on.

Steamlaunches were going to and fro, from ship to shore, all the time; and torpedo-boats were towing our small boats. I lost my platoon not long after we got ashore; but there were plenty of officers to follow. The Turks then retired about one mile inland, into positions they had prepared for occupation; and the bullets really did begin to fly. The Turks had about 20 machine guns, a battery of 18-pounders, and a couple of Howitzers.

I worked my way up to the firing-line (although I don't know how I got there, across the bullet-swept fields and hills). They were throwing shells, in threes and fours, all day. I would like to have a penny for every bullet that whizzed past my head that day. I saw a shell hit the ground about two chains in front of me. When it burst, it blew the dirt and stones up about 20 feet in the air. The shells that hit the men took half their body and their heads clean off. I saw some awful sights.

I was about a chain behind the firing-line when I got hit. I knew I would.

Private J. M. Wemyss (the son of Mr. A. C. Wemyss, of Carapooee) writes home after being wounded at the Dardanelles on April 26th.

No. 2 General Hospital,
EGYPT.
6th. May. 1915.

Dear Mother,

I am getting along alright and expect to go back to the Front again very shortly. You will no doubt have seen before this, from the papers, that we have been fighting pretty solidly. The papers will be able to tell you more of it than we can from here, but we have been cut up badly.

I don't think there are many of my "A" Company left that are not wounded or killed — officers and all. I do not know what it will be like when we go back to it again, but we had a tough job to tackle for a start!

We landed in the face of heavy artillery and rifle and machine-gun fire, up the side of a steep hill that was rough and scrubby (like monkey nuts). We could not see the enemy, although the Turks could see us coming — and they had cut down the scrub on the ridges and put up poles to mark the range of us as we came up the hill. We were to reinforce the Third Brigade who had landed the day before.

They played their machine-guns and shrapnel on to us with deadly results. But we could not fire back at them until we had got inland for about two miles. The scrub was no cover for us as their bullets seemed to sweep the ground just inches above the surface; but the job had to be done and somebody had to do it!

I don't think the Turks did much of a job on their part — they should have been able to shoot the lot of us as we came up to them. They did not like our bayonets and kept retiring from them. I do not know how they would have fared if the situation had been reversed and we had been in their position!

We were up at 2 a.m. on Sunday morning, waiting to land on Turkish soil. We were all ready by 4 a.m. but did not land until 6.30 a.m. We spent the waiting-time up on deck, watching our warships bombarding the Turkish forts.

Then we had a terrible time getting ashore in the small rowing-boats, for the forts were chopping shrapnel all around us like hailstones. About seven men were killed in my boat, and the boat behind us was absolutely riddled. A naval pinnace just got her to shore in time to save her from sinking.

When our boat grounded, we had to wade waist-high through the water to a very small beach. There was a gun-fort situated about 500 yards away from this beach, causing us severe damage. Then there were steep cliffs to climb, which I don't remember climbing; but perhaps I flew up them. Just on touching shore, my rifle was smashed with a piece of shrapnel, so I had to replace it with a dead man's gun.

When we got to the beach the sight was awful. There were bodies of our chaps floating all around, and the dead and dying were scattered all over the shore. You see, the 3rd. Brigade had landed one hour before us and had got a very hot reception.

I got into a couple of hot corners that Sunday. Our headquarters (to which I was attached as a despatch-runner) came under fire, during which our Adjutant and Major were hit, and several of our signallers were either killed or wounded.

Then, when I was delivering a message, I found myself with a party of about 100 men who were cut off and subjected to a murderous fire from rifle and machine-guns. But we hung on till sunset when we had to clear out — and only 25 of us got out of that unhurt. My mate, Dolley Burns (who is also home now) was badly hit in the legs during that stir.

Well, I managed to jog along until Tuesday when I got a bullet graze on the top of my arm — but that was only a trifle. I broke all of Postle's records during the next couple of days as I was running messages — and to get a message to the firing-line I had to run over a mile of open country which was infested with snipers, and I can assure you that their bullets had a habit of making me move fast!

I got hit on Thursday. I was kneeling down at the time and the bullet passed right through the back of my hand, fracturing a couple of bones and injuring a sinew or two, before striking me just over the knee. But, as luck would have it, I only got a nasty bruise.

After I got safely to the Hospital Ship I almost felt glad I had been wounded, for at last I knew that I could have a good sleep!

The following letter was written by <u>Lieutenant Charles Barrie</u> who was employed in the Colonial Bank, Donald, at the time he enlisted.

HELL ON EARTH

Alexandria Hospital.
7th. May, 1915.

Dear Mother,

I cabled you some days ago saying I was wounded. I thought, it best to let you know at once, and now you will be wanting to know all about it so I will do my best to tell you.

I was unlucky enough to go down on the first day (Sunday, 25th. April) after being in the fight for only six hours. What rotten luck! After eight months training to be knocked out in the first round; but it is no use complaining. The greatest wonder to us all is — HOW DID ANYONE LIVE THROUGH IT AT ALL?

The noise was terrible and the bullets were pattering around us all day just like hailstones they were, really! But we didn't mind them so much; it was the shrapnel we didn't like, and they simply peppered us with it all day long.

Shrapnel was catching the boats between ship and shore; and from then on, all day long, they were bursting all around us. Many a poor chap never even got out of the boat.

We had to force a landing, you know, against stormy opposition, but you will get details of the fight in the newspapers, I suppose. It is too long for me to tell you here, and all I will say further is — HOW PROUD WE ALL ARE OF OUR MEN.

It was their baptism of fire, you know, and such a one as probably no troops have ever received before; yet they fought like veterans, the discipline was splendid, and when ordered to advance there was no stopping them.

They didn't seem to know the meaning of "fear" and there was never a complaint from the wounded, though it was terrible to see the poor chaps falling down. The numbers of dead went up to <u>thousands</u> on the first day.

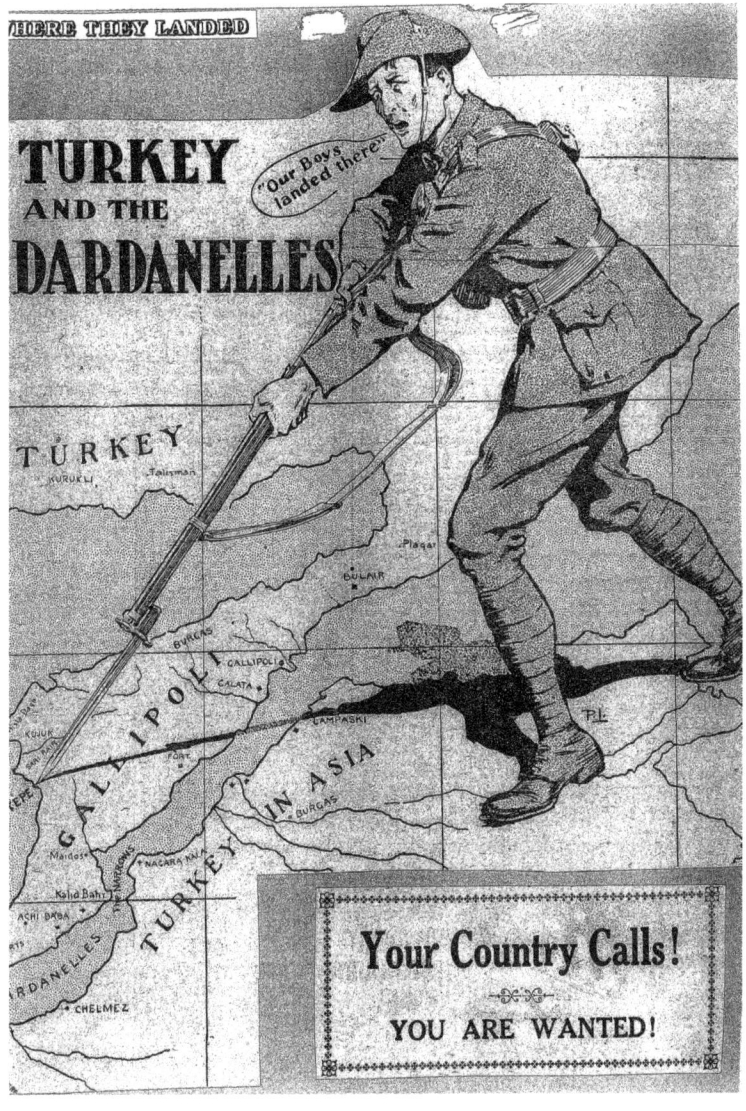

A BROTHER'S DEATH

<u>Private Reginald. Polkinghorne</u> (of St. Arnaud) must have found this letter very difficult to write. He had to tell his mother about the death of his brother, Private Clifford Polkinghorne.

Off Gibraltar.
7th. May, 1915.

Dear Mother,
This is a very hard letter to write, although I know you may be expecting it. You will by now have seen the list of the killed and wounded.

Clifford died a glorious death, a hero in the very front line of battle. Thousands of others fell that same day, Sunday, April 25th. Although it was full of glory for us who were fighting, it meant a lot of suffering to all of you at home.

It was a terrible fight, but not one of us shirked it at all. Indeed we were like old soldiers, the way we took the slaughter and bloodshed all around us.

Cliff and I were together all the time after he arrived in Egypt, and on the boat going to the Dardanelles. After we landed we were together for about ten minutes; and then we got separated. He was picked to go to the right, and I went to the left of our company.

We advanced and came under heavy fire at once. That was about 9 o'clock in the morning of the first day. After that, I never had time to took or think until after dark when we tried to re-form our company.

But only 50 returned, the other 200 being killed, wounded

or missing. Before morning, however, 26 more turned up, making only 76 out of our company of over 250. It was then the boys told me that Cliff was gone.

The fire of the Turks was so terrific that we could not get up to get Cliff until Tuesday morning. The boys did all they could for him. We buried him by himself in a grave on the hillside, just where the fiercest of the fighting had been .

Captain Coulter was very good and gave him a decent burial. The Captain read a service and all the boys who could be spared from the trenches came to pay their last respects to an honored comrade.

It terrible sudden, but still I am sure that Cliff was prepared for it. Captain Coulter asked me about you, and asked me to write as soon as possible. He had a brother killed beside him in South Africa in the Boer War.

Cliff's death was just the kind of death that a soldier wishes for. It is terrible to see those badly-wounded men lying around you when you cannot do anything for them.

That Sunday (April 25th.) was the hottest battle ever fought! The "Heads" thought we would retreat, in fact a retreat was ordered; but our General said he knew we would never retreat whilst there was one man of us left alive. So we held on and won!

The next three days and nights were just the same, only we had dug trenches, and so held the position. We had no sleep, and only a little bully-beef and biscuit to eat for the whole time.

The Turks actually crept up behind us because they dressed in our uniforms which they had stolen from the dead Australians. One of them shot me in the back on the Wednesday morning. It fair knocked me over!

The bullet went in just half-an-inch from the spine, just

missed my lung and stopped up under the shoulder-bone. When they took it out it gave a "ping" as it came from under the bone. Colonel Gartside was in my trench at the time and he had me sent straight-away to the A.M.C.

They took the bullet out and I was sent on to the hospital ship; and I am now sailing to England.

I know you will be grieving about Cliff, but do not worry. He died with many others, and their memories will be honored for centuries to come. We were against great odds that day. The Turks were 10 to 1 against us. They had artillery; yet we held our own and I think we beat them.

I am recovering now, but I have nothing left, not even my uniform; but I will get some in England. With Love, REG.

[Private Reginald Polkinghorne mentions Colonel Gartside. 7th. Battalion, who also died a hero's death the very day after this letter was written — on May 8th. He was shot down as he led his men up to the Turkish trenches in the great struggle for Krithia and Achi Baba.]

Private W. Tracy (of St. Arnaud) was another soldier from our district who was wounded in Turkey, during the Landing on the 25th. of April. He wrote the following letter to his father, Mr. T. Tracy.

Alexandria.   11th. May, 1915.

Dear Father,

"Just a few lines to let you know that we have landed into the firing-line, but I suppose you know by this time that we have been doing some fighting. I was among the unlucky ones.

I was shot in the back and the bullet went into the lung;

but I am getting on alright now, so don't worry about me. My wound is only slight but the bullet is still inside me somewhere and I suppose they will have to operate on me to get it out.

We lost about fifteen out of thirty of our officers. The Turks gave it to us pretty hot for a time, but I think we fared a bit better than some of the other battalions which they say were cut about awfully. I cannot give you any details of the fight because I never reached the firing-lines.

The Turks caught me with a bullet while I was still in the rowing-boat being pulled to the shore. I suppose they will soon patch me up, ready to stop another bullet. But I hope I may be a bit more fortunate next time — anyway, the Turks will not have such good cover by then.

I cannot tell how my mates got on for I have not seen any of them since they landed.

I met one of the Bliss boys (from St. Arnaud) on the hospital-ship as we returned from the Dardanelles. He was shot in the head and in the shoulder but he looked happy enough on it."

Private William Henry TRACY (7th. Battalion) was first wounded during the landing on 25th. April as he sat in a boat being rowed to shore. A bullet entered his back and lodged in his lung, but after his recovery in Egypt he returned to Gallipoli — and there was killed in action on 8th. August, 1915, in the fierce battle at Lone Pine when he was blown to bits by a bomb that fell into his trench.

LANDING STORES

Private F. L. Kay, son of Mr. G. Kay of St. Arnaud, writes to his parents from a hospital in Cairo.

12th. May, 1915.

Dear Mother,

I suppose you have read in the papers about the great fighting we are having at the Dardanelles. I will give you my movements for the past five weeks.

We left our camp at the Pyramids on Easter Saturday night, and marched to Cairo (about 10 miles) where we took the train to Alexandria, arriving there next morning.

We sailed from Alexandria on Easter Sunday night for an island called Lemnos, which belongs to Greece and is about 60 miles from the Dardanelles. We stayed at that island for two weeks, waiting for the troopships and the warships to get ready for the attack on the Dardanelles.

We left Lemnos on 24th. April about midnight, without

a light on any of our ships. We had breakfast at 3 o'clock in the morning, and then the warships started bombarding the forts. You could not imagine the great noise!

We at once started to land in small boats, pulled by the Naval tugs, which took us within 50 yards of the shore. We jumped into the water up to our waists and walked ashore under a shower of shot and shell.

Some of our poor fellows were shot before landing. We never waited for orders, but fixed bayonets and got into it. Although the Turks numbered 20 to 1 against us, they would not stand up against our bayonets.

By sunset that night, we had the Turks driven inland for about five miles from the shore. Though we were driving them back we were losing a lot of men. Our dead and wounded were lying everywhere.

When darkness set in we had to retire about half-a-mile to the top of a hill, where we started entrenching. The shrapnel-shells from the Turks were bursting all around us. We had no big guns with us as they were still on the ships.

The Turks made several attacks during the night, but we beat them back with the bayonet. By morning we were pretty well-entrenched. There continued a ceaseless hail of shot and shell from both sides. In the afternoon, our Battalion made a charge to take another hill, but how some of us got back is hard to tell; for the Turks turned about six machine-guns on to us and cut us up pretty badly. We lost several officers and our Colonel.

I was in the trenches from Sunday night till Thursday with nothing to eat and no sleep, fighting all the time. Our Battalion was relieved for a spell on Thursday; but we had only been out of the trenches a few hours and got settled down for a sleep (at last) when we had to rush away to help the men on our left flank, where the Turks were attacking very strongly.

I remained in the trenches until the following Wednesday — that was nine days' hard fighting. Never had a wash all that time, and very little sleep. I had the bad luck to get shot through the hand on Wednesday evening. I was, however, very fortunate for I had not been out of the trench an hour when a shell burst there and killed nearly all my mates.

I am nearly better now and hope to be back in the firing-line within a few days. I have not seen brother Tom, but I was told he was still alive on the day I was shot.

It is only three days' sailing from Egypt to the Dardanelles. We have had no news from the Front since I left there. I hope they have not killed all the Turks before I get back to the Front (where I hope to be in another week).

I suppose there would have been 6,000 Australians killed and wounded since we landed. There must be great anxiety in Australia just now and great excitement when they first heard we were in action.

We have had congratulations from the King. Lord Kitchener's last message was: — **"Stick to it, Australia. The world is proud of you. Sending you reinforcements. "**

If we had had another 50,000 Australians on the Sunday we landed, we would be in Constantinople by now. The Australians are the best fighters in the world. We have 2,000 English soldiers here with us, and they are always praising us. They think we are simply marvellous; and they say all Australians deserve a Victoria Cross each. The nurse just told me I am getting discharged from the hospital tomorrow.

Private H. Edelsten (of St. Arnaud) writes from Alexandria to his mother.

Dear Mother,

I have been in the firing-line for a short period at the Dardanelles. On Saturday, 1st. May, I managed to stop a bullet. One had just gone through the rim of my hat, but this one that hit me struck me in the right nostril and came out through my left cheek, near my ear. It was a peculiar sensation.

When the bleeding eased off, I made my way to the field dressing-station and my head was bound up. That night I was placed aboard the hospital ship with other wounded and sent back to Alexandra.

We are on a hospital ship now, and have been told that we are going to Southampton, in England. The wound does not trouble me at all, except that the left side of my face feels numbed. Otherwise, I am splendid.

Poor old Ossie. I suppose his people have had word of his death. He was killed two days before I was hit. He was shot by a sniper while having a wash and he only lived for about ten minutes. I was a few yards away from him at the time, but I did not know it was him until I saw our platoon officer holding up his head.

He was breathing his last when I reached him and the only words he spoke were, "I am hit in the back."

Another of my mates, Bert Widden, was killed the next day. Strange to say, he and Ossie used to sleep on either side of me in our tent at Heliopolis. I would like to tell you a lot more news, but I have probably said too much already as our letters have to be censored. I have seen Jack Parsons, Ted Murrells, Engelmann, Tracy and others.

Everything is fitted up lovely on this ship. It is an English hospital-ship with English nurses and doctors. The food and attention is splendid.

[Of the St. Arnaud boys mentioned here, <u>Sergeant Walter Engelmann,</u> was killed in action. Another brother, <u>Hubert Engelmann,</u> had died some weeks previously at Broadmeadows Camp from the dreaded Meningitis; so the poor parents suffered the tragic loss of two sons.]

STRETCHER-BEARERS BRING IN THE WOUNDED

(British Official Photograph)

IN PRAISE OF
STRETCHER-BEARERS

Stretcher-bearers, stretcher-bearers,
Running in the rain
Out amongst the flying shells
Seeking those in pain.
You carry in a wounded man
Then go out to seek again.
From danger's fire you never shrink,
Nor hide when others can;
Your work is far more deadly
Than that of a rifle-man.
Fatalistic, faithful, fearless,
You never crouched, but ran.
In sticky mud through sharp barbed wire
You searched where many fell;
Looking for a sign of life
In a bloody place like Hell.
Then run with him on your stretcher
To escape each killing shell.
Stretcher-bearers, stretcher-bearers,
To you our thanks are due.
You never shirked the danger
When there was work to do.
For we have seen and know your worth
And sing in praise of you.
F.B.

THE LAST MAN

George Lee joined the 14th. Battalion of the A.I.F. when the First World War began — and after several months of training in Egypt went to fight against the Turks on the Gallipoli Peninsula. Private Lee landed at Anzac Cove on the 1st May, 1915, and barely three weeks later was severely wounded in the knee at Courtney's Post.

Now, when Private Lee returned home after the war he told people how he had been saved by "the man with the donkey". Not only that, he claimed to have been the very last man rescued by the immortal John Simpson Kirkpatrick.

"I had heard of the heroism of Simpson and I certainly found it to be true," said Private Lee. "I fought with the 14th. Battalion, but was wounded when a bomb exploded in our trench at Courtney's Post. My leg was badly injured so I could not walk.

"Our trench was still under constant enemy fire when Simpson and his donkey suddenly arrived. He lifted me onto the back of his donkey and also helped another soldier with arm injuries to walk beside the animal.

"Simpson carried me on the back of his donkey down to the beach and put me into a rowing boat which then took us to the 'Galeka', an old vessel being used as a hospital ship. We had just reached the 'Galeka' when I was told that Simpson had been killed by snipers and I knew it must have been just after he rescued me. All the wounded soldiers on the ship were very upset when told of Simpson's death because he had saved many of them, too.

"I remember Simpson cursing the snipers as he walked his

donkey along the dangerous gullies down to the beach. He did not talk much as he was too busy rescuing the wounded. Simpson certainly saved my life, like hundreds of others, and I will never forget him, especially as I was the last man he rescued."

Simpson and his donkey "Duffy" ferrying a wounded man.

Shrapnel valley, on the 19th. May which was the very same day that Private Lee tells us he was wounded and there is, apparently, no other soldier who claims to be <u>the last man carried on Simpson's donkey</u>. That humble honour, without doubt, must be attributed to Private George Lee.

Everyone knows that John Simpson Kirkpatrick, with his adopted donkey, became a hero at Gallipoli whilst serving with the Australian army — yet actually he was an Englishman who had jumped ship in Queensland and worked there as a miner.

When war began he joined the Australian Medical Corps and landed on April 25th. at Anzac Cove with the 3rd. Brigade.

He adopted a lost donkey known as 'Duffy' and camped with this animal at the Indian mule depot.

Simpson used his donkey to carry injured men to safety, through rifle-fire and shrapnel, escaping death many times whilst doing such brave work.

It was on May 19th. that a Turkish sniper killed Simpson and he was buried on the beach at Hell Spit; but during those twenty-four days since the Landing on April 25th, Simpson rescued hundreds of wounded soldiers.

Interestingly, May 19th. was the very same day that L/Cpl Albert Jacka (14th. Battalion) fought bravely during a Turkish attack in Monash Valley and was awarded the Victoria Cross. This medal (the highest given for outstanding valour) should have also been awarded to John Simpson Kirkpatrick (the man with the donkey) who risked his life many times to rescue wounded soldiers.

Perhaps the British regarded him as a deserter because he joined the Australian army? Yet, if anyone deserves the Victoria Cross it should be Simpson who saved many lives at the risk of losing his own — and whose brave actions created a true spirit of comradeship amongst the soldiers at Gallipoli.

Was it not a donkey on which the Good Samaritan put a poor wounded Jew and took him to be cared for in the inn? And was it not a humble donkey on which Our Lord rode in triumph into Jerusalem to death and glory? This animal has now become a symbol of peace and love — and Simpson is known as 'The Anzacs Good Samaritan'.

The text carved on the statue reads:

SIMPSON HELPING A
WOUNDED SOLDIER TO
WHERE HIS DONKEY AND
ANOTHER PATIENT WAITS
CARVED BY JOHN BRADY
SEPT 1998

Statue at Lakes Entrance, (Victoria)

Canberra ~ Simpson and Donkey

COURTNEY'S POST 19TH. MAY 1915

It was 19th. May, 1915, at Gallipoli when Turkish forces eager to smash the Anzac invasion, charged down the heights towards the Australian trenches. They had about 40,000 soldiers and led by German generals they were eager to drive the Anzacs off their land. The day before the attack the Turks had sent a warning by Morse code which said, 'We will put you back into the sea tomorrow, you Australian bastards!" but this message certainly put the 12,500 Anzacs on full alert.

Eventually the Turks arrived, carrying bayonets and throwing hand grenades into the Anzac front-line near Courtney's Post, which was held by the 14th. Battalion. It was here that Private Albert Jacka played a key role in stopping the enemy's attack (and won a Victoria Cross for his brave action).

When the Turks were firing down from a trench above them, Jacka charged on his own straight towards the enemy and jumped into their trench with nothing but his rifle and fixed bayonet. Then he realized with horror there were at least ten armed and angry Turkish soldiers waiting to kill him.

Quickly, almost without thinking, Jacka raised his rifle, pulled the trigger and shot the nearest Turk. Then he reloaded and shot the second, the third, the fourth and with his last bullet he shot the fifth who fell dead on the pile. Jacka then leapt over the bodies and plunged his bayonet into a startled sixth Turk. Then he pulled the bloody blade out of that collapsing body with a clever twist before plunging it into a seventh Turk who was frozen with fear.

As he was about to attack the last three Turks he saw they all had their hands up in the air and were begging to surrender. At that moment Anzac reinforcements arrived and looking up from the trench at the officer in charge, Jacka, with his bloodied bayonet still pointed at the Turks, said, "I managed to get the beggars, sir!" <u>and this was how Private Albert Jacka became the first Australian VC of World War 1.</u>

The Victoria Cross is the British Commonwealth's highest decoration for conspicuous gallantry above and beyond the call of duty. During the First World War at Gallipoli and on the Western Front as many as 66 Victoria Crosses were awarded to Australians.

St. Kilda Cemetery

Lance-Corporal Albert Jacks, the first Australian soldier to be awarded the VC in the First World War

FROM GALLIPOLI

"I've a little wet house in a trench which the raindrops continually drench;
There's dead Turks all around, just polluting the ground,
And they give off a beautiful stench.
Beneath us in place of a door, there's a mat of wet mud and some straw;
Whilst the Turks' bullets tear through the rain-sodden air
T'wards my little wet home in the trench.
Their snipers who keep on the go always force us to stay down below;
And their star-shells at night are a soldier's delight,
But causes bad language to flow.
On dry biscuits and bully we chew, for it's days since we tasted a stew.
So with bombs here and there, no place can compare
With my little wet home in a trench."

CAPE HELLES

Sergeant Alexander Walder (of Watchem) wrote this account of his experiences at <u>Cape Helles</u>. (It was actually part of a bigger piece of writing which he later sent to his mother.) He was in the 8th. Battalion, 2nd. Infantry Brigade, which was selected to go and help the British and French capture the village of Krithia and the important hill of Achi Baba in the South of the Peninsula. This assault took place at the beginning of May, 1915.

Dear Mother,

A suggestion was made that the 2nd. Infantry Brigade could be very nicely used at a place called Cape Helles (at the toe of the Peninsula) to act as Reserves for the British and Indian troops who had already made a marked progress there.

So, on the night of <u>May 5th</u>, we were drawn from our dug-outs (at Gaba Tepe) and told to fall-in. Each man carried his gun down to the wharf where several huge barges lay in readiness to take us out to the Mine-Sweepers and Destroyers waiting in Anzac Cove. Very soon 200 willing hearts were stowed away on board the Destroyer, SCORPION; and after a three-hour run we found ourselves at the beach where the British Fusilier Brigade had landed a couple of days before us.

It was now 5.30 a.m. and the work began of unloading our equipment from the over-crowded SCORPION. Although there was scarcely time during our short stay on the boat to make the acquaintance of 'Jack Tar', we <u>did</u> receive delicious refreshments. There was hot soup, cocoa, bread, butter, oranges, biscuits and other delicacies that the sailors deprived themselves of for the comfort of strangers who had never before this moment set foot on their Destroyer.

Fortunately, the night was warm — as there was no covering to be obtained on the ship except our own Great Coats. Soon we were trudging up the cliff towards the battered village of Sedd-el-Bahr. We found a piece of unoccupied ground where a light breakfast was partaken and at 12.30 we received orders to pack up again and get ready to move on.

Our first indication of coming into enemy country was a long line of ammunition waggons that could be heard several minutes before they made an appearance. Suddenly, many teams of British gun-horses came rushing towards us along the road from the direction of the famous Achi Baba (a hill of twin peaks, stretching right across this part of the narrow Peninsula where the Turks are firmly-entrenched).

Khaki uniforms were predominant in this place; but several soldiers in light-blue pants, with a bright-red line down the side of each leg, made us realise that Frenchmen, too, were taking part in this great struggle. They were driving waggons drawn by mules, or grey Flemish horses. Last, but not least, we saw the Indian Transport soldiers, jogging happily along with their mountain pole-waggons and tough, little mules.

Moving off from our bivouac, we tramped down a gentle hillside and along a powdered white cart-track between groves of olive trees. Suddenly, an amazing specimen of Turkish trench entanglements met our eyes. It was a piece of ground, about 10 yards wide and 100 yards long, made into a dense cobweb of barbed wire; and inside these dimensions were 6 lines of strong iron posts with row upon row of carefully-dug, deep trenches. This gives you some idea of what an attacking party has to contend with! Yet from these strong entrenchments the enemy had been recently routed and pursued.

Now, on our right and overlooking the sea were two carefully-mounted, enemy siege guns of 13-inch calibre. These two monsters spoke out at frequent intervals, in opposition to British cruisers lying in the bay below; until the QUEEN ELIZABETH, by clever marksmanship, planted several 15-inch shells at the base of these monsters, thus putting both guns and crew out of action for the present.

The little village to the left of these guns was the next object of an attack. But it was well-prepared for our onslaught as a few thousand enemy soldiers showed a determined effort to hold it at all costs. Yet there was not the slightest hesitation on the part of any Australian, and once again the cold steel of our bayonets proved superior to their rifles. The fleeing mass of Turks retreated into the distance in hasty disorder.

A cable's length further on we passed the tragic result of a heavy day's fighting. It was a neatly-made grave with over 80 brave hearts lying within. This grave was on the left of the road which now led us closer to danger.

As we tramped that busy road, we met those who were returning from the Front and who were only too eager to give us details of what was happening there; and in another direction, many stretcher-bearers trudged along narrow, winding tracks with their living burdens. They would often call out, "Hello, chum, have you a hat-badge or button to spare to complete my collection?"

Before nightfall we reached our goal and once again began the job of digging our new home. We were surrounded by British and Indian troops, whilst the blue uniforms of the French were conspicuous among the dark foliage of fig trees on our right The Algerian infantryman is easily recognised by his dark skin and small cap; and he has a fine fighting reputation among the Allied Forces of the present day.

As darkness set in we were given our allotted spaces, and had only a few minutes to make a temporary, overhead cover from shrapnel — for it was feared the Turks could see us from the twin peaks of Achi Baba and would shell us. Some of our men were determined to complete the task of digging trenches, but on reaching a depth of three feet they hit an unlimited supply of fresh water. So then other dug-outs had to be constructed which would be more shallow, but at least dry.

Water occurred sometimes after only digging for eighteen inches, so we found that water was plentiful in this valley, and running streams were in abundance. We could have fresh-water baths now. instead of the "Briney".

The next day was spent here, so our time was taken up in searching for souvenirs of Cape Helles. In glorious weather we tramped around several lines of encampments, including the camp of our French brothers. They smiled pleasantly whenever a Colonial tore off his hat-badge and offered to exchange it for a similar novelty from a French soldier's coat.

In our diligent search that day, we found curios such as cartridges, bayonets, water-bottles, revolvers and many similar articles which we eagerly carried back to our camp. Sadly, they had to be left there, as no extras can be added to the burden on a soldier's back when he faces trouble. It was on the 8th of May, as we prepared dinner, that the whistle sounded. "Fall In".

At 1.30 p.m. a general muster was made and every man was eager to accomplish the feat that was before him. First, a left wheel; and then after passing over a number of ditches we found ourselves on the scent of the enemy. We trailed along a narrow path that led us to a spot which showed every indication of fierce fighting — thousands of empty cartridge cases lay scattered over the ground.

Further on we passed a line of happy Indians, who asked in broken English, "Are you Australia?" When each time the answer came back, "We are!" a hearty cheer would go up from those smiling, coloured faces.

Some 300 yards later, we met a line of Gurkhas with their bare heads and shining white teeth. They greeted the slouch hat with very excited cheers, and occasionally one would draw his knife and wave it frantically over his shaven head as much as to say, "Bring in the scalps".

Only 20 minutes after we passed these men, we reached a hollow, shady spot where, after a hasty afternoon snack, we erected a temporary shelter. This slight depression screened us from the enemy who could look down on us from Achi Baba. Then the order came to pack up and move on — where, we did not know.

We followed a winding creek that led us right into the Jaws of Death, for it was here that a great number of our boys were hit. We also lost our good adjutant (Captain A. H. Possingham) who fell, killed by a stray bullet. He was a fine officer who had gained the confidence of every Boy-at-Arms in the 2nd. Brigade.

As we advanced, our second-in-command (Lieutenant-Colonel Field) was shot in the jaw. At this point we received a fair amount of shelling, because, although we were four or five miles from the firing-line, the Turks were attempting to cut us off as supports. Our pathway along the bank of the creek was blown up, leaving only a rough track for us to take; this led us round to where the attack began across the open battlefield.

Prior to leaving this track, a number of our boys got hit

— and J. Stanbrook was struck in the left chest by a bullet which was afterwards found hanging in a piece of loose skin on his back. The bullet passed from front to rear of his brawny chest, only causing a temporary paralysis. He got up and with no assistance walked back to the Dressing-Station.

At 4.45 p.m. the order was given for the 8th Battalion to move, and every man was once again on the job! Only a hundred yards in front we came upon a thickly-clustered line of Tommies and Drakes in a trench. It was a strongly-held position, so we had a few minutes' rest there. But just as the Tommies were asking us where we were going, an order was passed along the trench for every Australian to advance.

We thought the officers had gone mad to order us forward, as the enemy was but a few hundred yards in front sweeping the ground with his bullets. The brigadier was up on the parapet saying. "Now then, Australians! Which of you men are Australians? Come on. Australians!"

No sooner said than done and the task of advancing began. With a yell and a cheer we burst from the last bit of cover we had, or were likely to get for a long time. Bullets were raining thickly as we left the 'Tommies' Trench" — and the history of war began to repeat itself.

Men were continually dropping as we ran straight towards the enemy machine-guns; and our line weakened as those machine-guns enjoyed the pleasure of mowing us down by companies. The advance continued, although it slightly wavered beneath such a great loss; then several of the Drake Boys, Tommies and Frenchmen came up beside us.

We had only gone a short distance of 300 yards, (one man falling at every yard) yet the worst of the fighting had hardly begun. The nearer we got (to Krithia and Achi Baba) the firmer became our determination to rout the Turk from his safe position. How he must have enjoyed the manner in which we were being slaughtered!

Undaunted, the Colonial Boys charged despite their terrible losses. Our line wavered slightly where huge gaps had been made. Did it occur to our Generals-in-command that such an event should never have taken place? Not in daylight, anyway, when we were such easy targets.

In that evening I saw some awful sights amid the suffering of hundreds that lay nearby; and before the night was out a thousand lay dead or wounded upon the open moorland.

As I lay on the ground, raising my head slightly for observation purposes and hoping to catch a glimpse of the way to advance, I saw the enemy retreating in wild disorder; yet at the same time we received the full force of dozens of Turkish machine-guns from our right. There was the bitter feeling of dissatisfaction which comes when the odds are ten to one against you, and when there is difficulty in getting the required number of support troops up to the front-line to fill in your gaps.

Another 100 yards had been gained, but only by adding many names to the Roll of Honour! We paid dearly for that little piece of ground we won. With every inch forward, we now began to meet a difficulty that would make even the bravest hold his breath. We were only 400 yards from the nearest enemy trench, so when the next 200 yards had to be won it was all done in one fast race — and so fast that many of us were carried along in the rush.

On reaching the limit, we were content to lie down and prepare our defence work in anticipation of a rough night. Some men had brought with them a spade, while others carried a cumbersome pick; and it was with these implements that our cover was dug, quickly and systematically. Without these weapons our delay in making cover would have added to the Roll of Honour and probably left none of the 2nd. Brigade to tell the tale!

Darkness would favour the Turk, as being on the defensive and safe behind his guns he had nothing to worry about. We could see his rifle flashes in the dark all along the Turkish line and realised that his snipers were again active. At 8 p.m. our trenches were ready to provide us with a substantial covering for at least one night and day; but it was in the course of their construction that I got a smack from a stray bullet.

I started out to make my own way to the beach, which was about 5 miles from our present position. Those who could walk were certainly the lucky ones. As I returned, the battlefield was filled with the cries of the wounded, and I could hardly go ten yards in any direction without coming upon them. They could do nothing for themselves and I was too helpless to give a helping hand. Many had been hit in the stomach or intestines — the most painful kind of wound, and from which very few survived.

The only time I found I could be of some use, it proved worthless because, as I was carrying the poor fellow along, he received a second bullet that rendered him lifeless and sent him to his last resting place. Often I came across groups of 20 or more of the wounded, lying huddled together — though some were <u>not</u> wounded, sorry to say! Our dead heroes lay in pitiful heaps — and hundreds of voices could be heard in all kinds of painful tones.

It was during this day's work that we suffered the loss of such fine men as Captain Possingham, Colonel Gartside and many other notable Lieutenants in the 2nd. Infantry Brigade."

[War historian, C.E.W. Bean, records the death of Colonel Gartside. It seems that, having been hit once, he was rising again to lead a further rush upon the enemy trenches, saying, "Come on, boys, I know it's deadly, but we must get on," when he was struck in the abdomen by machine-gun bullets and fell, mortally wounded. C.E.W. Bean also writes that the patience of the wounded around the "Tommies' Trench" was astonishing. As they lay craving for water, a soldier, carrying a supply to the front-line, poured a little into a mess-tin, explaining that the rest was needed "for the boys in the firing-line." One after another the wounded and dying merely moistened their lips with it and then passed it on so that there might be enough for all.]

Sergeant-Major Hal. Young (of St. Arnaud) writes to his parents from Cape Helles where the 2nd. Infantry Brigade was sent on May 6th. to help the British and the French in an assault on Krithia village and Achi Baba. Dear Mother, *May, 1915.*

We are not allowed to write much. We have been having a rough time and have been in two big engagements. Poor old Colonel Field was shot in the jaw. He was from Castlemaine. I lost one of my best friends in Sergeant Hart, who was shot dead near me.

The first day we landed, I got a crack on my thumb by a shrapnel bullet, but it was nothing, and it is better now. We had good sport in the trenches shooting snipers; I got six of them in three days. One I shot at 950 yards, so my shooting practice is coming in handy again.

The sailors on the British war boats are great chaps and get on well with us. The Frenchmen, also, are very good to us. We got a loaf of bread and some coffee from them last night. It's a change after hard biscuits and tea!

We did look pretty sights after being in the trenches for five days. Never had a wash or shave all that time. It rained one night and, of course, that "improved things" as we were mud from head to foot. I can tell you, the South African war was only child's play compared to this.

It is a miracle how one escapes the rain of bullets that fall around us. Give my love to all, as I cannot write to everyone. We have not had any mail here for five weeks, and we are dying to receive news from home. Young Ted Murrells was wounded in the leg — also Bill Harris (who used to go shooting rabbits with me).

This is a fine country we are in (at Cape Helles) with grass and water everywhere. Springs are found all over the place. It is a pity to see war destroying such a beautiful place.

One sees some awful sights, but we are used to it now. I have just got word that I am promoted to Sergeant-Major, quite a rise for me. Best of love to all the folks — HAL.

Corporal THEO BLISS (5th. Btn.) was wounded on April 25th. at Gabe Tepe. He is writing from Mena Hospital, Egypt, on 21st. May, 1915.

Dear Mother,

I got one on the top of my scalp (shrapnel from a shell) and about half-an-hour afterwards, or an hour, I got a bullet in the shoulder (right) and almost immediately another piece of shrapnel struck me on the same shoulder and tore the flesh for about 7 inches over the top of where the bullet went in, but never did too much damage. The doctor took the bullet out of my shoulder on the second day out at sea, on the hospital ship when returning to Alexandria.

I am pretty weak at present through having lost such a lot of blood; but as my shoulder blade was only splintered and not broken, I was very lucky. I am rapidly regaining my strength.

My word, it was a veritable Hell on earth, and I sincerely hope it will not be the same again. All the officers and men who have been in other wars say that they have never experienced the like before and don't suppose they will again.

We had to fix bayonets in the small rowing-boats from which we landed, and jump into the water up to our chests, and then charge out on to the beach where the Turks and Germans were waiting for us in their thousands. They were pouring bullets into our boys like rain.

Dozens of our lads never got out of the sea on to the beach, but were shot down in the boats, or in the water. We drove the enemy up the first mountain (it is very mountainous country here in Turkey) and they ran screaming like a lot of pigs, back into their trenches — and then they poured down bullets and shells and machine-gun fire into us.

But we drove them back and had pushed them inland about four miles when I got shot. I and another mate (Ted Kimpston of Donald) who was also shot in the head, helped one another back to the beach where the Army Medical Corps were roughly dressing all the wounds.

It took us three hours to get back four miles — sliding down mountain sides on the seat of our trousers, and then crawling up the other sides on our hands and knees. Somehow, we got down into the mucky trenches in the valley. Here we had to walk up to our knees in soft, dirty slush — and both of us just about played out!

I had fainted five times as I was losing blood all the time. My puttees came off in the mud, and I have not seen them since and never will. I lost everything but my coat and pants and boots and cap; every other blessed thing gone, and now they are away up in the hills of Turkey.

Private H. Edelsten (4th Brigade) **writes from a Birmingham hospital to his family in St. Arnaud.**

30th. May, 1915.

Dear Mother,

I am doing well. We embarked at Alexandria for Lemnos Island on April 11th. and arrived several days later and were in port there for over a week with dozens of other troopships and warships.

On the morning of April 25th. we could hear the boom of the British Navy's big guns in the distance. It was at that very moment the British troops were landing at Cape Helles, while the Australians were similarly occupied at Gaba Tepe.

We, who were attached to the 4th. Brigade, realised that the bombardment of the Dardanelles had started in real earnest and we would soon know what it was like to face ball-cartridge and artillery-fire. Yet all hands were quite happy and looking forward to the forthcoming campaign.

We arrived opposite the heights of Gaba Tepe towards evening and could quite distinctly hear the din of the battle that was proceeding on shore between Australians and Turks. We were quite excited and anxious to get ashore and help our comrades.

There were four Companies on the boat, but only two were taken off that night as reinforcements. We stayed on deck and looked at the steep cliffs and hills where the gallant 3rd.

Brigade had landed. We could scarcely realise it was possible for troops to land in such a rough place where the enemy were waiting, fully-prepared, without getting completely annihilated. Yet the Australians accomplished this feat, although at a great sacrifice of lives.

When the 3rd. Brigade got near the shore, they jumped out of the boats (some of them were up to their necks in water), fixed bayonets, and with an Australian yell they made a dash at the Turks; despite. the machine-guns and rifle-fire which were making awful gaps in their ranks.

The Turks would not wait for a hand-to-hand encounter with the bayonet. Australians took the high ridges, one after another; and then they had to dig themselves in and hold them.

I never had a shirt to wear until I got here to Mena, as my other shirt and singlet were cut off me — both being saturated with blood, and my arm had gone painfully stiff and I could not bend it.

Turkey is a beautiful country, and to look across those lovely hills and valleys and then think of all my dead and wounded comrades, it's hard to imagine how God (le bon Dieu) would allow it. But it's not for me to say, and He knows best.

Well, it is a fortnight today since I got shot, and yesterday I used my wounded arm for the first time; it had been strapped to my side for 12 days. But I'm right again now, and as soon as the scabs dry up I'm off to Alexandria for seven days' rest in the Rest Camp there.

It seems as though I am dreaming sometimes, to find myself back in Egypt again, among the niggers and their dirty habits.

One of our 5th. Battalion Majors was killed (Major Fethers) — also two Company Officers, three Sergeants, one Corporal and about eleven men were all killed just in my Company.

The word "SPHINX" means "living image" of a god, or of a divine king. This "GREAT SPHINX" is in the form of a couchant lion, with the head of a Pharaoh wearing the royal head-dress and with the snake on the brow. Between the front paws is a tiny temple, discovered by Caviglia, in 1816.

DARDANELLES BOMBARDED
BY BRITISH FLEET

The following letter is from a Donald man, <u>Mr. Richard</u>
<u>Milburn,</u> who writes to his brother, Mr. Jos. Milburn. When
the war started in August, 1914, he Joined a British ship, the
H.M.S. SOUDAN, and patrolled the North Sea, with the
Grand Fleet. When he was on duty in the North Sea (at the
time the Germans raided the East Coast of England for the
second time) Mr. Richard Milburn had the pleasure of see-
ing the BLUCHER sunk — and helped to take the German
survivors on board his ship. Then his ship was sent to the Dar-
danelles in February as part of the British Fleet, to bombard
the Turkish forts. He says: -

"While our ships were firing, we were rather too close to be
comfortable — several shots from the forts came quite close
to us. During the first three weeks in the Dardanelles, our
casualties were about 200, of whom we had 170 wounded on
board. It was four weeks before we left for Malta, with 220
wounded. So you will see that our casualties were small for
the great work we had on hand. I would like to have known
the Turkish losses — they must have been very great.

After discharging our patients at Malta, we returned to
the Dardanelles, and were there when the OCEAN, IRRE-
SISTIBLE, and the French ship, BOUVET, were sunk. We
(Britishers) were very lucky, as there were about 750 sailors
in the crew on each of our two ships yet we only lost 7 men;
while the French lost about 560 men out of their crew of 800.

Subsequently, we returned to our base and remained

there until Sunday, 25th. April — the official landing of our soldiers on the Gallipoli Peninsula. Ours was the first hospital ship to arrive that morning (about 6-30 a.m.). We were not two miles from the point where S.S. RIVER CLYDE was beached, carrying 2,000 troops on board, who were ready to land when they got the chance.

All our other troops were towed to the shore by tug boats, in small life boats — from 40 to 50 in each. The sight I will never forget! To see our brave soldiers making a dash for the shore through a hail of bullets. It was wonderful how they ever got there; and then they charged up the cliffs, stopping at nothing.

All the time our battleships covered the advance of our troops with their big guns, keeping up a very fierce fire all day and night. The noise was enough to deafen one. Our work started very soon. At 7-30 a.m. we had the first boatload of wounded arriving alongside us, and by 5 p.m. had 500 wounded on board. We then moved off and transferred our patients to a hospital carrier.

We then went back to the shore (where the Australians and New Zealanders landed) and again started taking in the wounded. Soon we had 400 of our boys on board, and took them to the Malta hospital which is two days' run from the Dardanelles.

I must mention about our Australian boys, the way they took their wounds. It made me feel so proud of them. Not a word about pain, joking among themselves, quite happy. All that worried them was, how long would it be before they could get back to the fighting line?

I met a Bendigo boy, Alex Robinson, who knows you all and wishes to be remembered. I have had a letter from him since he left my ship at Malta, stating that he was pleased to be going back to the firing line in a few days, so I wrote and wished him the best of luck. Our hospital staff consists of 19 surgeons, 4 sisters, 64 naval ratings; and our crew is 178 all told."

Sergeant Alexander Walder

EXTRACTS PROM MY ORIGINAL DIARY OF THE GALLIPOLI CAMPAIGN IN 1915.

(SERGEANT ALEXANDER WALDER, OF Watchem)

Sunday —
April 25 1915.
Under fire on the boat, shrapnelled as we landed and got it hot and strong ever since. The wounded were on our boat even before we were off it. The 3rd. Brigade landed and presented an ugly picture, as their losses were so great.

Monday —
April 26
Turks are still pouring in shrapnel — and every kind of bad bullet is in use. A sad tale is to be told out in the Front line. QUEEN ELIZABETH is giving them Hell and we have guns to compete against theirs. Our rifle-shooting is good and the boys laugh when a Turk falls on the point of their bayonet. Last night they did not charge us although they were only 50 yards away; the Turks are a bit shy of the bayonet.

Tuesday —
April 27
A full day of artillery and rifle fire with a few of our boys wounded and killed. Captain Cooper shot a spy last night. The bullets are like a packet of crackers going off. Four days and four nights in the trenches without sleep, yet we have to relieve 'D' Company today. Our boys are holding out well against great odds.

Wednesday — April 28 A quiet day with occasional shrapnel from the Turks, but our guns give them 3 to their 1. Shells land in our dug-out and enemy snipers are busy, yet we catch them. Hundreds of their shrapnel have fallen out of range, but a few boys killed.

Thursday — April 29 Another day's fighting, as well as all night. We have not had a day's rest since we landed, but last night we had half-an-hour of sleep in the cold. Charlie Orr turned up safe. Their guns are being beaten and their infantry routed. Shells burst beside us, over us, underneath us, and all around us. They have not made a good stand with the bayonet yet, but they would stand no chance against our boys. Daily rations are the usual hard biscuits, bully-beef, tea and sugar.

Private Vincent O 'Brien writes to his mother in Birchip: -

Heliopolis. 1915.

"You will see by the address that we have
left Mena Camp (and the desert sands)
and are now in a much better one. We are
camped on the Heliopolis race-course, only a few minutes'
walk from the train line, and much nearer to Cairo than we
were before.

There are some splendid buildings here, more like civilisation — except for the niggers' quarters. The population is
practically all European. They have a Luna Park and skating-
rink just a few minutes' walk from our camp, and there are
picture-shows and musical entertainments everywhere.

I suppose you heard the news of the Australian forces
having landed at the Dardanelles on 25th. April, and they've
been in pretty hot water since. There are wounded Australians arriving here every day to the Heliopolis hospitals. The
receiving hospital is near here, in a huge building that used
to be a very big, expensive hotel. The buildings at Luna Park
are also being used for the wounded.

I was up at the hospital and met one of the Forresters from
Curyo. He has a bullet wound in his arm. Arthur Forrester
was a tent-mate of Harry Smythe (Berriwillock) and he told
me that Harry was not injured when he got his bullet — but
goodness knows how Harry has been getting on since then.

The infantry landed at Gallipoli first. The artillery and
machine-gun division, ammunition column and other corps
have been landing ever since.

The Light-Horse seem to have been left out of it somehow.
Our regiment are the "Jonahs" (like Jonah, in the Bible, we
are complaining because we are forgotten and ignored).

All the other Light-Horse regiments are leaving their horses behind and are going (dismounted) to join the infantry. Our fellows are kicking up a 'devil of a shine' because they wouldn't let us go on foot and get in amongst it. We are properly fed-up with this training and looking after horses; anyway, it's getting too infernally hot to be in the stables. After all, I think the "foot slogging" is the best; it's such a terrible drag being tied down to the horses. Anyhow, it's the infantrymen that get to see the fighting, not 'review' soldiers like us.

Our Colonel is always telling us what a great name we have, but what good is that to us? A lot of darned "red tape" and foolery is just about all one can call it. Some of us were thinking of clearing off and going with some other corps to the Front, but it is pretty difficult to do; and if we are caught we would get put in the "clink" and perhaps never fire a shot.

I heard that some fellows who deserted, and tried to get off to the Front with another corps, were discovered and brought back and got six months' detention; and are now going to be sent back to Australia as a punishment. It's a bit hot, isn't it?

Another youth and I have answered applications for the military Post Office in Cairo, sorting the mail. Young Viv. Shepherd, from Birchip, is there and he says I will have a good chance of getting the job. The Post Office employees have their meals and accommodation at the National Hotel — so it would be a change from camp life.

I am so used to sleeping outside now, and I am eating well and getting quite fat. In fact, everyone seems to have put on weight since they joined the forces. Although we are always kept going, and have a rough time, it seems a lazy life; we never have any real hard work. I know which I would rather do! Monotony is harder than labour.

But if I do get this job at the Post Office, I will leave it and get back in the squadron as soon as my regiment leave for action at the Front. I like our squadron very well; the officers are all fine fellows. Our Major and Captain are both fine men; we all think a lot of them. I wish the whole regiment had the same kind of officers throughout and perhaps we would be in action by this time.

We have just about all <u>Colac</u> men in our troop. Some of them know dad's people. I will be able to write to you more often if I get in the Post office. We were told that this regiment would not be leaving for a considerable time yet. I hope you are all well, as I am at present. The "lights out" has sounded, so I will have to close."

[Vincent O'Brien's keenness to join the infantry at Gallipoli is an example of the courage of our men. He did <u>eventually</u> get the chance to leave his horse behind in Egypt and join the men at the Front. Sadly, he had not been long in the trenches before a bomb burst near him and a piece of shrapnel entered his knee Septic poisoning set in and his life was in danger. To save his life, doctors had to amputate his leg above the knee. After the operation, he made a good recovery and returned home to Birchip (minus one leg) at the end of January, 1916]

ONE OF AUSTRALIA'S HEROES

Before the war, Lance-Corporal Alexander Gillies was known as one of the most active men in the Victorian police. He could deliver a punch with his "straight left" when action against a criminal had to take the place of words. His famous punch was known to amateur boxers (as well as to evil-doers) around Victoria. But tragically Constable A. A. Gillies lost that strong, left hand in the trenches at Quinn's Post.

It happened on May 29th. when Turks broke into Quinn's Post and much heavy fighting took place before the enemy could be driven out. Lance-Corporal Gillies (5th. Battalion) was leading a little body of men in one of the first charges when he was stabbed by a Turkish bayonet on the inside of his left thigh.

He made light of his wound and, having bound it up with a dead man's puttees, he limped onwards to duty once more. Almost immediately afterwards, Gillies was wounded again when a piece of shrapnel entered his chest, passing under his heart.

A following shell burst beside him, carrying away his left hand and breaking a splinter off his hip bone. Gillies did not realize his hand had gone and he attempted to staunch his wounds unassisted. Then he became weak from loss of blood.

Nearby was another wounded man and the two became friends, although neither thought to ask the other his name. "I'm hit, mate!" was the informal introduction from the stranger (a soldier of the 6th. Battalion). Gillies answered, "Me, too!"

The two men helped each other as far as possible and shared the contents of their water-bottles. The bullets were still whistling overhead when a stray shot injured Guilles in both knees. The two comrades crawled to a spot where a small rise in the ground offered some protection from the enemy — and there they lay from 1 o'clock in the afternoon until the sun went down.

Being now out of the area likely to be visited by stretcher-bearers, Gillies and his companion set out to crawl on hands and knees to a Dressing-Station somewhere behind their lines. On the way they passed a clump of low scrub, and, when almost level with it, a machine-gun began to fire at them from its concealed position.

The two men sank down on their faces, thinking that it was a foe hiding behind the scrub. But a few minutes later a soldier stuck his head out through the bushes; and when he saw the two wounded men lying there in the moonlight, the colourful language he used established beyond all doubt that he was an Australian, too.

When he saw their terrible injuries the stranger hurried off to bring assistance; but he never returned, so Gillies and his friend struggled onwards again.

Later on, they passed a dead body upon their track that seemed strangely familiar — it was the man who had gone for help.

It was 11 o'clock at night when the wounded men continued their painful, slow journey; and by good luck they came upon an Australian trench where they sheltered until daybreak.

Here they were found the next day, carried to the beach and placed on a hospital transport.

Using PERI-SCOPE rifles in the trenches

THE DEATH OF OSSIE WEMYSS

Dear Mother,

Next morning we were taken ashore, and it was then we had our baptism of fire. Every time our troops attempted to land, the enemy shelled the shore with shrapnel — which bursts everywhere and causes much damage.

While on the way to reinforce the firing-line, some of our men were wounded. That night we set to work to dig out a supporting trench; and eventually we dug a communication trench into the firing-line so as we could come and go with safety.

On Wednesday night, April 28th. we were relieved by an English regiment and we inarched back to the beach in the dark; and then had to stand to arms all night as an attack was expected along the shore.

Next morning we had a bath in the sea, followed by a shave. It was while this was going on that poor Ossie met his sad end. He had gone down to the water's edge and had just stooped down to wash his hands. It was hard luck to get killed in that way; but dozens of Australians have met the same fate — shot by snipers while on the beach or when travelling along Shrapnel Gully on their way back to the firing-line.

On the afternoon of May 1st. the Turks made a determined attack on our position. Out of the eight of us who were in an observation trench, six got shot in the head and four were killed. I got hit under the temple near the left ear.

The wounded left Alexandria on a hospital ship on May 8th. bound for Southampton. We got on splendidly until near Gibraltar, when in a thick fog an Italian merchant ship crossed our bows — perhaps she mistook the light on our ship for a lighthouse. The sad result was that the Italian ship sank with several lives lost. Our boat had a narrow escape and we had to stay in Gibraltar for two days while temporary repairs were effected.

Ossie's last words to his mate, Hartley Edelsten, were, "I'm hit in the back." He died ten minutes later.

Lieutenant Hal Young writes a letter to the "St. Arnaud Mercury."

GALLIPOLI.

June. 1915.

"Just a line to let you know that most of the St. Arnaud boys are well. Young Kell was wounded, not killed as first supposed. Reddie Wyatt was shot in the leg. Charlie Alexander got a flesh wound in his leg, also, but it is not serious.

Arch Mills, from Conooer Bridge, was shot in the neck, the bullet coming out at his side. He is getting on fine and will soon be back with us. He was shot on the first day we landed. We were all sorry, as he had carried a wounded man on his back, under an awful heavy fire. It happened when 20 or 30 of us had been cut off by the enemy and we had a job to get all the wounded back. Young Ted Murrells, in the 6th. Battalion, was also wounded in the leg, and Don Nicholson in the arm.

I have been in two of the biggest engagements here, and never want to go through another like the last one. It was awful, but we gained the position which is the main thing I suppose. Captain Ebeling, of Avoca, is well; and deserves the highest praise. He is one of the coolest men I ever saw under fire, and the men think a lot of him.

I have left my old regiment (the 8th. Battalion) and have been transferred to the 7th. Battalion, with the rank of 2nd. Lieutenant. I did not like leaving my old mates, but of course I could not refuse promotion.

We get plenty of shell-fire here, the shrapnel being the worst. I got a crack on the thumb the first day we landed, but it was nothing serious and soon healed. At present we are having a spell out of the trenches and it is great to get a dip in the ocean and a good shave. We are no "oil paintings" I can assure you after being in the trenches for five days.

We have dug-outs and live like rabbits, especially when a shell comes our way. It is wonderful the miraculous escapes men have! Five of us were having breakfast the other morning when a shell burst right over us, wounding four men in another dug-out. One piece of the shell went through one of our rifle-butts, and another piece through our water-bin on the ground right beside us. Of course, we got a lovely shower-bath.

One cannot help smiling sometimes at the mad scramble a shell makes. I saw rather an amusing thing the other day. We were down bathing when we heard a shell coming. Of course, all of us rushed for shelter; but one chap just sat on the sand with a towel wrapped around his head. We all thought it very funny. It was only natural for him to try and protect his head, but what good a towel could do I cannot see.

We have some good sport at sniping the enemy. I got six in two days; one at 950 yards. One of my best mates was shot dead by their snipers, so I think I avenged his death. All St. Arnaud boys send regards."

Private Andrew Leslie Muir (of Donald) writes home to his mother.

June. 1915.

We have just landed back from the Dardanelles, after having had a fight with the Turks. We are having a rest-spell in Alexandria for a month. I think we will be going to England after this, but we are not quite sure yet.

We had a terrible fight with the Turks, and others are still going to the front while we are having a spell. It was terrible to see the dead and wounded, and your mates falling alongside while you still keep going. I lost my two pals on the first day, and I was left without a scratch. They were blown to pieces and many others with them.

I am, however, still going strong and hope to hear from you soon. It is very hard to get our mail. It is held up for a long time. How are all the folks at home? Tell Taylor it is good fun here, and it would do him good to see it.

I don't know whether this note will reach you or not, but I hope it will, as we will soon be back in the fighting-line again. I am keeping well and hope to be home by Xmas if all is well, but I think not. We are having a fierce fight for it this time, and it is pretty hard.

Private Joseph Hoare (14th. Battalion) writes from Golgosh to his parents in Donald.

THE AUSTRALIAN IS BETTER

"I'm getting a few letters from home now and am glad to see that you are all well. As for myself, I could not be better. We left Heliopolis about the 3rd. April and came to Alexandria by train. Then we sailed across to Lemnos Island where we had a couple of weeks doing "Landing Practice" from the boats. It took about three hours to get us to the Gallipoli Peninsula from Mudros Harbour.

That Sunday saw our first taste of fire, and I can tell you — it was warm! But the boys stuck to it like glue, and after a soled scrap we got a lovely frontier. We gave the Turks a good betting. They have had a big shake-up all along; but I cannot tell you how many men we have lost. However, their losses were about 8 to 1 of us.

Opposing trenches in places are only about 30 yards apart, and at times it's a bit hot with hand-grenades. I got hit on the head with a piece of shrapnel, but it never hurt much. I was laid out for a couple of hours but was none the worse for it. Watts was wounded — but it is not bad.

We are out of the trenches for a spell, and it is very enjoyable, too. I have had as many as three consecutive nights in the line, but feel none the worse for it. I cannot describe our great fight when we landed, but you will have read the gist of it in the papers — it was awful! I heard that J. Cantwell was shot through the hand on the first day, and that Ged. Pearce is in hospital.

My 4th. Brigade had a bad time on landing — under the enemy guns, artillery and rifle fire — and I do not know how I got through it all. I had a few close calls, but I am really just a joke. One day, I had my gun 'split open' in my hand, so that was close enough for me.

We have now dug in, and taken up a position here that all the

Turks on this earth cannot shift us from. We are simply holding it until more of our boys can go in from the other side (of the Peninsula). I cannot say how many men we have lost, but I know that the enemy lost more men than we did.

On the 18th. of May there was a furious bombardment, and then on the 19th. of May the Turks made an attack on our position. Several new divisions of Turks (under Field-Marshal Von Sanders) attacked us at dawn; and they boasted that they would drive us into the sea or lose the Ottoman Empire. But instead of that happening, they lost so many men that they pleaded for a 24 hours' Armistice to bury their dead — at which we were glad to give them a hand!

The Turks lost about 10,000 men in the attack — and our losses were comparatively few. That was the day I had the gun 'split open' in my hand; as well as being laid out for a couple of hours. The scrap lasted for 34 hours, and we have taken all the sting out of their tails. They realise now that the Australian is better than they thought.

Well, for myself, I never felt better. We are getting plenty of work (when we are not busy in the front line) digging trenches and making roads — just the thing to keep us fit; so you need have no fears about my health. I eat tike a horse.

I can imagine the proud feelings of our Australian people when they read of the work done by our fellows here. It cannot be over-estimated, and we have been nick-named "The White Gurkhas" by the Naval men and the Turks. The Indian troops think the world of us.

Well, it is now time to go to my "Bully Beef and Biscuits" before work. So I am signing off, with kindest regards to Donald. — JOE."

[It is said that, as the Turks retreated after their great assault on the Australian lines, an Aussie voice yelled after them, "Play yer agin next Saturday!" <u>Private Joseph Hoare died in action on August 20th.</u>]

A BIRCHIP LAD

__Gunner Alf Power__ of Birchip, writes again to his mother; this time from a war hospital.

Luna Park Hospital, HELIOPOLIS.

1915.

My wound has nearly healed and I will be able to go back to the Front in about a fortnight's time. I got news of brother Walter the other day. I saw a chap that was with him in a bayonet charge. He said Walter was up in front the whole time. After the charge, their officer asked for volunteers to go out and kill some snipers who were making things very hot for our men.

Ten men went out — Walter among them. They got a very rough time, and only two men returned. Walter was one of them; and he was helping a wounded mate back into the trenches. The chap I was talking to, said the last time he saw Walter he was cleaning his rifle in the trench. He said he did not see Walter after that as he got a bullet in the leg himself and had to leave the firing-line. Don't worry, Mother, about Walter, as he will come through all right; he has the luck of a Chinaman.

We have lost an awful lot of men up to date, killed and wounded. Of course, hundreds of them will go back to fight again. Our casualties are about 30,000; that includes the French and British regular troops. There are twice as many British and French troops in the Dardanelles as what there are Australian and New Zealand troops. The war will soon be over now that Italy is into it. Remember me to all the folks around.

Mr. and Mrs. POWER, of Birchip, had <u>four sons</u> who volunteered for service at the beginning of the Great War. The eldest son died on the voyage to Egypt with the First Convoy — and was buried at sea. He had caught the dreaded pneumonia — which was so infectious in Australian Army camps. The second and third sons, Alf and Walter (as you have heard in this letter) were collecting scalps at Gallipoli. Alf was wounded and returned home some time in 1916. Their youngest son, Gordon, also caught pneumonia and died in the Birchip hospital while home on weekend leave.

"FIX BAYONETS!" then "OVER THE TOP!"

Here is the filth and stench of war.
The corpses on the parapet.
The maggots on the floor.

THERE IS NO PLACE
LIKE AUSTRALIA

Private J. Pasini writes to his mother. Who lives at St. Arnaud North.

Heliopolis Hospital,
EGYPT.
6th. June. 1915.
Dear Mother.
I am not too bad. I stopped a bullet after fighting for four weeks. I got it in the back, below the right kidney. It did not go right through; if it had, I might be a cold soldier now.

Brother Peter is alright, as far as I know. He was in the trenches when I was hit on the 26th. May.

A big crowd of us were in the sea swimming, and the enemy started firing shrapnel. I escaped the bullets from the first shell, got out of the water fast and sheltered under the bank of a hill. I was hit when the next shell burst.

The Turks fire shells on the beach every day. and hit a lot of the boys. But we need to swim to wash off the lice!

The day before I was hit, seven of us were lying on the side of the hill for a rest We were dog-tired, having been in the trenches for 48 hours without any sleep. Well, a shell burst close by, and three of those on one side of me, and two on my other side, were wounded — some very badly — but I escaped.

The previous night the Turks charged at us from midnight till noon the next day. What with the machine-guns, rifles and artillery, the hills around us fairly trembled.

The Turks came at us in their thousands, but they could not get into our trenches. As fast as they approached, they were shot down. The officers told us it was a great victory for us to keep them back.

They came at us and we were outnumbered, ten to one; but that's the way we like them to come so we can mow them down in hundreds.

A man's life is valued at <u>nothing</u> in this war! You are shot down like rabbits, and all one thinks about is how to kill the enemy. We had dead bodies by the hundreds, right up to our trenches, left lying there for a month. The smell was getting terrible.

The Turks wanted four days to bury their dead, but were only given nine hours. Our men and the Turks worked half-way between each other's trenches, and buried all the dead bodies they could in that short time. The Turks were not allowed to come nearer than half-way to our trenches (which were well-manned because the Turks are a treacherous lot).

Our wounded men are well-looked after here. We all think of home as there is no place like Australia. The letters are brought to us in the trenches when we are in the firing-line. It livens a man up to get a letter from home. I will write again before I go back to the Front.

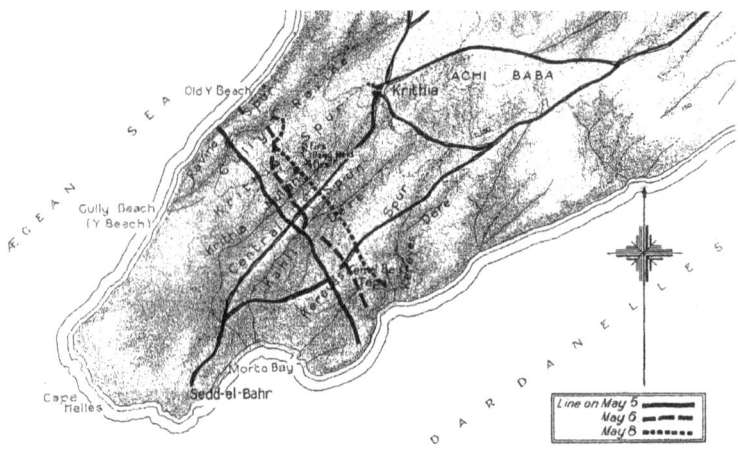

The Cape Helles area, showing the advance of the Allied army towards Achi Baba in the Second Battle of Krithia, 6th. 7th, and 8th May, 1915

HORIZONTAL lines show the advance of the British, Australian, New Zealand and Indian troops up the Peninsula from Sedd-el-Bahr, during the 6th. 7th. And 8th. Of May in 1915.

Sapper Rogasch (of Marnoo) wrote the following letter to a friend:

but in July this brave soldier lost his life at Gallipoli.
"DON'T JOIN THE INFANTRY"
GALLIPOLI.
　13th June. 1915.

"I have seen that big super dreadnought, QUEEN ELIZABETH, with her 15-inch guns. It is a wonderful ship and an admirable spectacle to gaze upon. She has to stand 7 or 8 miles out from the coast so that her shells will clear the hills; and when she fires it is even more deafening than the loudest thunder. Where her projectile hits, it makes a hole 50 feet in diameter. Her shell weighs nearly a ton!

We have also seen about 50 other ships, French and British, with 13-inch and 12-inch and all other calibre of guns, down to a 10-pounder (which is about a 3-inch bore). They make deafening reports when they go off, these big guns.

Well, we left Mena Camp (in Egypt) on Easter Sunday, and after an uneventful voyage reached Lemnos Island (near Greece) on Friday, 8th. April. We spent about two weeks there, practising boat-landings. We left Lemnos on the 24th. April and arrived at our place of disembarkation on the 25th. April.

Everywhere, we could hear the warships playing havoc with the enemy fort and batteries along the Gallipoli coast. The din was deafening. We stepped off our transport and filed down a gangway onto the deck of a destroyer. It was much quicker to use a gangway instead of the rope-ladders on which we had been practising for two weeks! Near the coast we climbed down from the destroyer into rowing-boats and, when they were full, a steam-pinnace towed us all the way to the shore.

We had to jump out of the boats into the water and wade to the shore. As we were doing this, a shell flew about three feet above our heads, but fell into the sea. This was our first taste of war! I soon learnt that shrapnel is the most dangerous of all shells because it bursts and sends forth hundreds of bullets, any of which has a death-dealing blow for 200 yards.

Well, I was that surprised at the suddenness of it that I took no notice, but the next shrapnel found me well and snugly-hidden from danger in a big hole on the shore. We soon got to work making roads and other engineering works; while all the time, shells (about sixty to the minute) fell around us.

Such was our life during the seven weeks here; it is just a repetition of danger, with a few rest-spells in between. I have been hit twice with shrapnel; once behind the right ear (which for a few hours gave me a stiff neck) and then three weeks later, I got hit on the right arm. Luckily, it was only bruised.

You can hear a shell coming a good while before it gets to you, so you have time to get out of the road and under cover. The shell-bursts are a beautiful sight (like fireworks) especially at night. At first, everyone used to duck, but now, little or no heed is paid to them — except by newcomers whose antics under fire, for a while, are the laughing stock of the ones that came before them.

I would advise anyone who is coming to the war to join the Engineers, or the Army Service Corps, or the Artillery."

Sapper Edward Albert George ROGASCH was killed on the 27th. June, 1915, whilst in a tunnel that was being dug under No Man's Land at 'Lone Pine'. The Turks exploded two mines nearby, so the tunnel collapsed, burying him alive.

An Indian Cavalryman (Photo — Sergeant A. Walder)

Gallipoli Trenches

A SOLDIER and HIS MASCOT

A Gallipoli Trench

(Photo: Gunner Geddie Pearse)

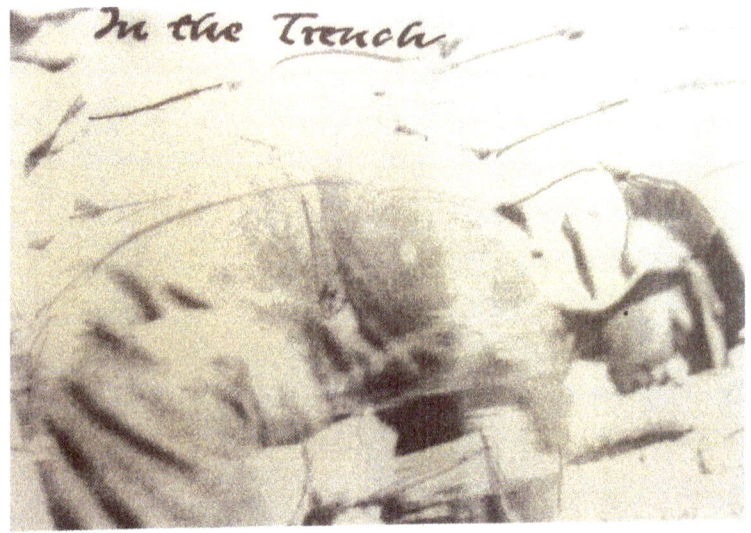

Writing a Letter

Dugout in Gallipoli

Rest Gully

7th. Btn. Soldiers beside their tent.
Photo — Gunner Geddie Pearse

Corporal George Bowden (*of Carron*) *writes to his father, prior to leaving Australia. He has two other brothers serving at the Front.*

Dear Father,
<u>June 15th. 1915.</u>
I am just writing you these few lines to let you know that we are sailing almost immediately for England. I did not expect to be going for at least two weeks, but tonight (Thursday) we got orders to sail on Saturday. I intended to obtain country leave and run up and see you, but I cannot do that now.

However, rest assured I will not forget that I am the son of an Englishman, and I hope to give you a chance of being proud of me. You have given your three sons to fight for old England, and no man could do more, and you are made of the good old stuff which made England what she is.

I ask you as a favour to the three of us, not to worry about us, but keep your heart up for all our sakes and look for our speedy return; for if we thought you were worrying about us we would be miserable, as you know. Nothing could deter me from going now, as I consider it my duty to England, to Australia and to you, to go and do my little bit.

Candidly, I do not think we will ever see the Front. By the time we do another six months' training in England there will not be much fighting left to do, so console yourself with that.

Mother is taking it well. She firmly believes that we will only get a free trip out of it, but if we do get any fighting I hope we will be a credit to our father and mother.

I will write to you at every opportunity after we go away. We will be well out to sea by the time you get this letter. I do not know whether brothers Jack and Dug have written to you or not, but if they have not, this will answer for the three of us. I cannot think of anything else to write about now; so, Father, I will say "Goodbye", with best love from your loving son, George.

Private <u>Norman Liddle</u> writes from Gallipoli to his Donald friends, Mr. and Mrs. Bert Basset.

9th. Battalion, Mediterranean Forces.
15th. June. 1915.
"I received your so welcome letter yesterday and I was so pleased to hear from you. I have been wondering if you had forgotten me, but still I thought I would get a letter from you sometime or other.

Well, Bert, no doubt you hear of our whereabouts daily as you will see our doings in the papers. We have had a pretty hot time — but I have been fortunate so far. We get plenty of shrapnel etc. One has to live like a rabbit in a dug-out There's always plenty of excitement and one sees strange sights at this game.

We have plenty of Battle Ships here with us but they leave us at times on account of hostile submarines. One of our Battle Ships was torpedoed right in front of our eyes and she went down in twenty minutes. She had done such grand work, too. Our boats' bombarding leaves a nasty taste in the enemy's mouth.

Well, Bert, I will be able to tell you a dose of news when I come back. I just hope this year turns out to be successful. I wish you would send me a Donald paper as reading material is scarce here. I will write to you again first opportunity. Please remember me to all my friends in Donald."

[This unlucky battleship was the H.M.S. TRIUMPH. *She*

was hit at noon on <u>May 25th. 1915.</u> by a torpedo from a marauding Austrian (or German) submarine which had crept unnoticed around the Gaba Tepe promontory. H.M.S. TRIUMPH turned bottom upwards and sank under the eyes of <u>both</u> armies as many Turks and Australians on the hillsides looked down to watch this awesome sight. Thanks to a nearby destroyer pressing against her listing side, most of the crew were saved. A Turkish battery on the cliff-top began to fire at the little rescue-boats; but suddenly the guns stopped and there was absolute silence as the huge battleship slipped from sight beneath the waters of Anzac Cove. Two days later H.M.S. MAJESTIC was similarly sunk off Cape Helles, possibly by the same submarine.

Gallipoli Peninsula
A LIGHT-HORSEMAN

Trooper Alexander Andrews BARBER (8th. Light Horse Regiment) died from his wounds on 22nd. June, 1915, after a hand grenade burst beside him and pieces of shrapnel hit his head, arms, hands, stomach and legs. He suffered for six hours before succumbing to his terrible injuries.

STRETCHER BEARERS at GALLIPOLI

A TRUE HERO

Here is a true story from Gallipoli that involves an Australian and a Turkish soldier and was told many times in a Cairo Army Hospital. It describes a dramatic wrestling match on a cliff top on that rugged Peninsula.

Two sworn enemies unexpectedly came face to face on top of a cliff at Sari Bair whilst each man was doing guard duty for his company. At once they sprang at each other, knocking the rifle out of each other's hands.

The Australian wisely did not attempt to regain his fallen weapon, but instead closed with the Turk hoping to throw him over the cliff by using sheer brute strength. However, the big Turk was his match in height and weight and a fierce struggle took place as each man endeavoured to gain the upper hand.

Their wrestling match intensified as they reached the edge of that high cliff, for each man clung like grim death to the other. Suddenly, the fragile ground beneath their feet collapsed and they both fell over the cliff and down into the sea.

Clinging to each other in a tight embrace, those tenacious antagonists fell hundreds of feet until they disappeared from view beneath the surface of the Aegean Sea. When they reappeared it was obvious the Turk could not swim for he was thrashing about helplessly in the deep water and gasping for breath.

The Australian must have been a strong swimmer because he soon got the upper hand and quickly clutching the Turk by his throat held him under the water until he drowned.

Sadly, our Australian soldier did not survive the war. He was fatally wounded in a battle which occurred soon after this incident, but many of his mates lived to tell the dramatic tale about how he conquered the enemy.

Gus proudly wears his uniform for this studio photograph
(taken on the 9th. August, 1916)
'Gus' was severely wounded in the leg at Gallipoli.

Private Richard Allan writes from Gallipoli to his parents at Donald.

Dear Father,
27th, June. 1915.
Have only received one newspaper since leaving Australia. I have met "Weary" *(his brother)* and he is looking well, although he was very bad on the trip over. He often comes up to see me as we are camped not far apart.

We have had more experiences of the Turks' shrapnel as they have been shelling the beach fairly constant of late. I have a good dug-out and run for it when I hear shells coming.

We are still holding our own, and I think the Turks are getting done as they refuse to attack us. Our aeroplanes are flying over us as usual, but we have not seen any German aeroplanes lately, until yesterday when they dropped discs with type-written circulars inside.

I have been in the hospital for a fortnight, but am progressing well now. I am attached to the beach-party, and I am the "babbling brook" (cook). At first we had 50 men in the party, but now there are only 35 — the rest having gone down with sickness.

The French and British troops who are at Cape Helles (about six miles from us) have done some marvellous work and are advancing across the Peninsula steadily. The Turks' losses have been very heavy.

The British battleship LORD NELSON came here the other day and bombarded the Turks. You could hear nothing but an uproar of "Hurrahs" from all the boys on the hill. They are very pleased to see any of the enemy trenches bombarded by the ships and it seems to put new life into our boys.

I have had a hot time in the land of the Turks. On the first day of landing I was hit on the hand, but it did not make much of a wound so I kept going.

On <u>May 19th.</u> the Turks attacked us heavily, but were badly defeated and lost about 7,000 in an area of about three acres. The next morning we could see nothing but dead Turks around us!

It makes one laugh to see from 300 to 400 Australians bathing in the sea and ducking when the shells lob around them. Some of the shells are 11.2 inch.

The cooking on the beach has to be done at night, owing to the shelling which is going on all day. Sometimes 100 shells will be fired without hitting anything because they fall into the water. The QUEEN ELIZABETH's shells make the Turks run out of their trenches, and then our boys can knock them over.

SERGEANT NIVAN NEYLAND

The Turks performed many cruel deeds at Gallipoli. Wounded Australians left in their hands received no mercy; and sometimes the Turks would brutally kick them and roll them over a cliff. Other captives were shot, or bayoneted. A few were sent to dig tunnels in the Taurus and Amanus Mountains, but these mostly died within a year or two from the Turks' barbaric treatment.

Captives who ended up in Turkish prison camps rarely survived. However, one prisoner who returned to tell the world of his experiences was Sergeant Niven Neyland, of Corack. He enlisted in the 14th. Battalion which consisted entirely of Victorian men; and after training at Broadmeadows Camp he embarked for Egypt and then Gallipoli.

He was badly wounded in 1915 during the August offensive when the Turks launched a heavy attack upon Australian trenches. Niven and his brave little band desperately fought to hold their position until most of them were killed and only then did the remaining thirteen surrender to the enemy.

Although Sergeant Neyland had been shot through his neck, the Turks dragged him outside and placed him against a tree. He was told to renounce his king, or they would shoot him. Three times they threatened him and each time he refused; so they said they admired his courage and allowed him to live.

During the following three years he received terrible treatment whilst in Turkish hands and by the time this brave young soldier was repatriated in November, 1918, he was a very sick man and a shadow of his former self.

Private J. H. Tierney (Army Medical Corps} writes from Gallipoli to his mother in Watchem. Private Tierney has since been wounded.

Dear Mother,

3rd. July. 1915.

I'm still going strong, having managed so far to duck the fight when danger is in the air. A "Jack Johnson" burst near me and gave me a dousing of dirt; a narrow escape, certainly, but a miss is as good as a mile. The Turks have another new gun which we have christened "Whistling Rufus" because its shells create a whistling noise when in the air.

Today our aeroplane is over the Turkish lines endeavouring to locate "Rufus" for our artillery; but "Rufus" is like Brer Rabbit — "lays low and says nuffin". Nevertheless, this is a game of chance and the odds are 100 to 1 against us. It is marvellous how so many escape the shells. I have seen a 35-pounder drop among at least 30 Red Cross workers, and only one was injured — and then not seriously. Machine-guns are the most severe death-dealing devices here.

At present as I write, the Turks are firing shrapnel at our aeroplane — which is dropping bombs — but she is too high up and out of their range. Still, we can hear the whirr of the propellers.

The Turkish aeronauts are afraid of our naval guns. There is a plane on the beach here, once the property of the Germans, which the QUEEN ELIZABETH shot down. Achi Baba is still being bombarded, and the destroyers are doing excellent work.

The British destroyers are very fast and as soon as a shot is fired, they flee and bombard another place. It is magnificent to watch a mammoth battleship coming up at full speed.

The smoke from her funnels is like a bush-fire (nothing but smoke), and the spray created by her bow resembles flames.

I saw the whole fleet rush up when the ill-fated TRIUMPH met her end at the hands of a submarine. A destroyer chased and fired on the pirate, but the latter escaped.

We have just had a new issue of clothes, and we get ample food here now — such as fresh beef, bacon, cheese, biscuits, jam, onions, tea, sugar, pepper, salt preserved potatoes, and also cigarettes. But matches are pretty scarce and wood for fires is scarce.

All the Watchem boys are well. Those who stay at home do not know what they are missing. Of course, the game is risky, but it has its compensations.

A combined letter to the St. Amaud newspaper, from <u>*Private W. McNicol*</u> *and* <u>*Private A. Dunlop.*</u> *(of the 2nd, Brigade) is very descriptive and comprehensive. One can just imagine these two Anzacs, sitting outside their dug-out in the Gallipoli sunshine, constructing the following lines for the information of folks in their home district.*

<u>10th. July. 1915.</u>
"It is now nearly twelve months since we left old St. Arnaud, and, though we as infantry have had a pretty rough "row to hoe" right through, our experiences of the last couple of months will long be remembered.

We are not in the firing-line at present, however, though the Turks are giving us fairly frequent reminders of their presence by sending shells and shrapnel among us. We are in dug-outs on the side of a hill facing the Aegean Sea, and after our work is finished we have a fair amount of time to ourselves; so, thinking you might find space in your columns, we decided to write a brief account of our experiences since leaving Mena camp, in Egypt.

The order to break camp at Mena was received with great jubilation by us, as we were eager to try our hand with Johnnie the Turk. We left Mena and proceeded to Cairo, where we entrained for Alexandria. We arrived without mishap.

With two companies of the 7th. Battalion we moved out on the transport-ship into the Bay; and after being anchored there a couple of days, orders to proceed to our destination were received. After an uneventful trip we anchored in a bay off Lemnos Island where we stayed for nine days, during which time we went ashore on a couple of occasions to do skirmishing-drill. Everyone on board was anxious to be "up and doing", and when the order came to start on the final stage of our journey everyone on board was in the highest spirits.

We arrived off the coast of Gallipoli on <u>Sunday. April 25th</u>. and anchored until daybreak when destroyers came alongside and we filed down the gangplanks on to them. From these destroyers we were put into barges, which were then towed ashore by steam-pinnaces.

We landed successfully, though the Turks gave us plenty to think about by pumping lead into us from machine-guns and rifles, and the bursting shrapnel was enough to inspire terror in any man. The support of our British Naval guns was grand, and the work of the gunners on the BACCHANTE, TRIUMPH and QUEEN ELIZABETH (as well as other boats) went a long way in helping us to land.

Having accomplished a landing we pushed inland for a short distance and formed a firing-line on the right, near the Turkish stronghold of <u>GabaTepe</u>. Here we lay exposed until dark when we began to dig in; and we had established ourselves in a fairly strong position by 8 p.m. The 3rd.

Brigade was on the left, the 1st. Brigade in the centre, while we formed the right flank. The New Zealanders landed later and formed up on the extreme left. At 9-30 the Turks made their first attack on our new position.

Shouting their centuries old war cry of "Allah! Allah!" and with a great blowing of bugles, they advanced through a standing crop of tall wheat, which made it hard for us to discern them. When they were within about 100 yards of us we opened fire, and at this comparatively short range our fire was very effective.

They still advanced, however, till within about 30 yards of our position, when they were forced to retire. They made three attacks on us that night, but all were repulsed and the enemy's losses were heavy. Although the sight was an unaccustomed one to us, it did our hearts good to peep over the parapets of our trenches in the morning and see the heaps of dead Turks, lying where they had fallen during the charges on the previous night.

Our second day, <u>Monday 26th. April</u>, was fairly quiet until the evening when everyone rejoiced to hear the sound of our own artillery — which, owing to the rough nature of this country, had been unable to get up the hills before this time. The fire of our artillery, together with the fire of the big guns of the British war-boats, created an indescribable din; and their shooting created havoc in the Turkish trenches.

About midnight we were subjected to another attack, but this was repulsed easily. Owing to our landing on the steep hills we had the Turks fogged. If we had landed on either side of the hills (where they expected we would) we would have met with an elaborate system of barbed wire entanglements etc. and, consequently, our job would have been a much harder one and our losses more serious.

The engineers were also of great assistance to us in clearing the way and making roads etc. And another thing for which we have to be thankful is the wholesome dread with which the Turks view our bayonets. Though they are good fighters, they will not stand against the sharp, cold steel fixed on the end of our rifles. Small blame to them either.

After a couple of days, matters were: comparatively quiet; and after five days in the trenches we were relieved. For two days we rested on the beach, and then we went back to the trenches again.

We improved our position in the saps etc. for 7 days, when we were once again relieved; and had just fixed ourselves up nicely in our dug-outs on the beach when our battalions of the 2nd. Brigade received orders to proceed to CapeHelles — which was a strong position held by the Turks on the extreme south of the Peninsula. The French, English and Indian troops had already effected a landing there, and we were being sent to act as reinforcements to them.

We were taken to our destination on board a mine-sweeper and sailed down the coast to the toe of the Peninsula. We arrived at CapeHelles early in the morning on May 6th. After landing we had a rest for two days, encamped about a mile and a half behind the firing line. The British troops, who had done good work since landing here, were now fighting about 3 miles inland.

On the afternoon of May 8th. we advanced in the face of heavy machine gun, rifle and artillery fire. In spite of the oppostion, however, we steadily advanced and formed a new firing line some 900 yards in front of the one held by the English troops (known as the "Tommies' Trench").

Our line was now extended diagonally right across the Peninsula — we being in the centre, New Zealanders on our left, and French on our right, with the Turkish trenches 400 yards in front of us! We held this position for seven days, during which time we were subjected to almost continual sniping by the Turks (at which they are experts, by the way, as many a good man knows to his cost). A violent bombardment upon Achi Baba (that double-shouldered hill which stretches across the width of this narow Peninsula) was carried on throughout all that time.

We were relieved by the East Lancashire Fusilliers; and, after a rest of a couple of days, those of us who had been lucky enough to come safely through this trying ordeal were shipped back to join our own troops again at GabaTepe.

The 2nd. Brigade was camped behind the firing-line; and we now had to go up in support to the firing-line every fourth night, as well as work in fatigue-parties on the beach during the day.

On May 25th. we witnessed the sinking of the good old battleship, TRIUMPH, by a hostile submarine. When she was struck, torpedoers, destroyers and trawlers rushed to her assistance, and rescued many of the crew; but the grand old TRIUMPH herself was a mortally-stricken vessel, and after keeling over slowly she gradually sank, firing deadly shots to the last.

It was an awe-inspiring sight, and our hearts were heavy as we watched the last of the brave ship that had done so much for us. We are now employed near the beach, making hand-grenades. Although we are not in the actual firing-line, there is still enough lead flying about to remind us that the war is still in progress."

McNICOL and DUNLOP

<u>*Lieutenant Hal. Young*</u> *(7th. Battalion) writes from Gallipoli to his St. Arnaud friend, Herbert Edwards — who has already left home to join the King's Light Horse Regiment in London.*

<u>*13th. July. 1915.*</u>
Dear Bert,
Australians had an awful engagement on the 8th. May at Cape Helles. The 2nd. Brigade was sent to take part in the attack on Achi Baba, a double-peaked hill which commands the Narrows. I consider this attack was worse them the one on the day we landed at Gaba Tepe because at Cape Helles we had to advance about two miles over level country, without a bit of cover, and then dig ourselves in whilst only 400 yards from the Turkish positions;

We all carried a pick or a shovel. I carried my shovel in front of my stomach, and this saved my life as it was hit by bullets three times. George Wardley was with me all the time and we dug ourselves in together. Poor Walter Engelmann was shot dead about this time.

The cries of the wounded were awful, but the Turks also lost terribly heavily. I had some great sniping — and on the morning of May 12th. I accounted for two of the enemy.

One was a Turkish officer who put his head too far over his parapet.

This war is proving which man is the most valuable — the good or the bad shot; In the trenches during the day-time, there is hardly a movement in the enemy's lines. We fire at the loopholes in the parapets and it takes a good shot to put a bullet through. A captured Turk stated that a terrible lot of his comrades had been lost owing to being shot through these loopholes. The Turks think the Australians are wonderful shots.

I have now been promoted to the rank of Lieutenant from the 29th. May and I am in the 7th. Battalion (D Company).

Private James BOOLEY (14th. Battalion) was. killed in actionon 8th. August, 1915, in that brave attack on Turkish positions at Hill 971. Before enlisting he worked for many years in Donald as a train shunter.

Private James Booley "Donald Mail" newspaper.

Gallipoli to the
July. 1915.
"Just a line from one of the Donald boys in this part of the world (Turkey). Well, things are fairly warm over in this country in two ways: the weather and the Turks!

The days are hot, although the nights are nice and cool, and the Turks are fairly warm with their shrapnel and Jack Johnsons. It is fairly hilly here, the hills being several hunded feet high, so chap is not too fresh when he gets to the top.

Joe Hoare is attached to the same Battalion as myself, also Albert Allan, who arrived with reinforcements a few days ago. George Wardley and Ged Pearce, of the 8th. Battalion, are still O.K. Jack Cantwell and Theo. Bliss are back with us again. They were wounded on the first day they landed. We have been here nine weeks, and it seems a very long time. Our homes here are in the ground, and are called dug-outs. A man learns to do a lot for himself when he takes on soldiering.

We had the first five weeks in the trenches, and it was not too pleasant at first as the nights were very cold, and we had no blankets or overcoats. We had to drop our packs when we landed, and we did not see many of them again.

We get plenty of fatigue-duty, but one has to do all classes of work in the army. Our food consists chiefly of bacon, cheese, jam, bread — and fresh meat is issued occasionally; but we get plenty of bully-beef with spuds and onions at times, and then we make up some dry hash.

We get four packets of cigarettes and one box of matches weekly. The matches are very scarce here. We have plenty of bathing, as we are camped near the beach; but the Turks put plenty of shrapnel on to the beach so swimming is very dangerous. I must close now, with my kindest regards to all the Donald folk."

Three unidentified members of the 24th Battalion taking a break in a trench on the Gallipoli Peninusuia.

British warships were withdrawn to safe harbours and were no tonger able to maintain a constant bombardment of the Gallipoli Peninsula. The bombardments by the British Navel Artillery was much appreciated by Australians in the trenches; but, in fact, the Navy's high-explosive shells mostly flew harmlessly overhead and did little actual damage to the Turks in their deep trenches. Against deep trenches (and machine-guns) the British Navy could do little damage really, for fear of killing thir own men. In fact, the Turks deliberately dug trenches <u>close</u> to our men for this reason.

H.M.S. Majestic, May 1915
This is one of the most remarkable photographs of the war,
showing the British battleship "MAJESTIC" in the very act of
sinking in the Dardanelles.

On the 29th. June the Turks attacked a position on Russell's Top held by the light horsemen with the result that many

Turks were killed and many wounded, whilst the 8th. and 9th. Regiments suffered just a few casualties. Our soldiers were jeering the Turks as they advanced with their bayonets — and the .light horsemen fired upon them from the parapets of their trenches. They jeered the Turks and encouraged them to come on, but what made them really mad was a Turk who yelled, "We will finish you Australian hopping kangaroos". It was after this attack which was a disaster for the enemy, that Major Deeble took a revolver and cartridge belt from a dead Turkish officer.

Photo — Gunner Geddie Pearse

Smoke from the ships' guns at Anzac Bay.
Photo — Gunner Geddie Pearse

Death in the Trenches

Corporal J. D. Freedland writes from Egypt to a Donald friend, on 16th. July, 1915.

DODGING THE FLIES

"Just a little letter, my first from Egypt, and probably my last as we are expecting to leave any time now. We landed at Suez and came North to Cairo by train, thence to here (Zeitoun Camp) which is ten miles from Cairo and the same distance from Heliopolis.

We had a splendid trip on the way over, and it took five weeks exactly. We had one funeral on board — the poor chap died from sunstroke. We are in the midst of the desert here and it is as hot as Hell; yesterday it was 116 degrees in the shade — though, of course, there is actually no shade to speak of.

We drill from 6 a.m. to 9 a.m. and then spend the rest of the day dodging the flies and the heat. There are not many men in camp here, as nearly all fit men are at the Front; but there are about 20,000 horses! As for the war, I suppose you see most of the news in the papers (but only the news that the public are meant to hear).

There are thousands of wounded men here, and all the hospitals are full up. I have seen lots of my mates wounded; but, alas, there are some mates I'll never see again. It's a case of war to the knife, and no quarter asked or given.

All Turks, unless wounded, are killed off-hand and we meet a similar fate, so a fellow had better not get captured! The Turks mutilate and butcher our wounded, and also our ambulance men — so now the latter are armed just the same as if they were ordinary soldiers.

The second day we arrived, they wanted five men to complete a unit for the Front. I volunteered and was accepted, but my officer at the last minute would not let me go. Stiff luck, but I hope to catch up with the Turks, as we expect to leave daily.

As for Egypt itself, it is beyond me to attempt to even describe it. It is a wonderful place — a queer mixture of things ancient and modern. All sorts and conditions of humanity mingle, and it's a great joy to go sight-seeing.

I'm seeing everything it is possible to see in the time; but money is really tight as we only get paid one shilling per day aboard ship — and I've had no pay since we landed ten days ago.

By the time this reaches you I expect I'll be "fighting some". I hope I don't stop too many bullets as "enough is as good as a feast". However, if I get plugged I hope to go under fighting like a man!"

<u>Gunner Alf Pouter</u> returned home to Birehip after his wounds prevented him from returning to the Front. He apoke of his experience to an audience in Bichip on 12th. August, 1915.

"I was quarter-master on the Star of Victoria when the war broke out. My ship was then off the Canary Islands and we received word to alter our course 200 miles west in order to avoid raiding ships. I arrived in Melbourne on 3rd. September, and 16 hours later had enlisted and was in camp at Broadmeadows.

I sailed with the 14th. Battalion on 22nd. December, and arrived at Alexandria six weeks later. Our only escort was submarine AE2; since lost in the Dardanelles. I remained in training at Heliopolis until April 12th. and then put into Lemnos Island where we spent eight days in practising landing movements. We could hear the guns firing 45 miles away.

There were over 400 ships at Lemnos Island, consisting of allied warships, hospital ships and transports. The QUEEN ELIZABETH was also there. We started to creep out at 2. 30 a.m. on <u>April 25th.</u> — the landing party (9th. Battalion) being aboard the H.M.S. QUEEN.

The landing-party landed at the place arranged near some cliffs. Suddenly the Turks sent up star-shells, which was followed by a burst of rifle-fire from the hill tops. The warships then commenced a bombardment, which was replied by Turkish batteries on shore. Men were then landed as fast as possible; they fixed bayonets in their boats and Jumped into the water in order to charge.

The 3rd. Brigade was first ashore, followed by the 2nd., 1st., the New Zealanders, and then the 4th. Brigade of which I was a member. Just before we landed, orders came for every man to re-embark, as the authorities thought it impossible to hold the position. But the men refused to retire, and, consequently, reinforcements were sent on.

The boats containing the 7th. Battalion attempted to land in the spot chosen, but got caught in barbed wire entanglements in the water, and were killed to a man by rifle and machine-gun fire. Volunteers were called for to bury the dead, and my section went. We found them all in a mutilated condition. It was the worst job I have ever had.

My section was then ordered to take the guns and get into position on the left of the New Zealanders. We were holding a position four miles long and three and a half miles deep, and Turkish shells were falling a mile and a half out to sea. Whilst going up "Shrapnel Gully", a shell dropped amongst my company, and slightly wounded seven men. I got a shrapnel ball in the right-leg puttee, but was not wounded.

On Monday, 26th. April, we got a shot at the Turks. Orders came that an attack was expected at daylight, and for every man to stand to arms. I was No. 2 on the right gun, and the Turks advanced en masse on the left flank. When they were close, orders were given for rapid fire. Heavy fire continued until 10 a.m., the Turks lying dead all along the line, while we had a number of casualties.

About noon we had our first casualty on the gun, No. 1 being shot in the head. I had to take his place — and intermittent firing occurred until dark; but their attack was repulsed. The noise from bursting shells was terrific. About midnight our first meal was served in the trenches, consisting of hot tea, boiled bacon and biscuits

At daylight, we were ordered to make an assault on a Turkish redoubt, close to the front of our lines. A heavy bombardment by naval guns preceded the attack, and within an hour we had captured the position, and made preparations to repulse any counter-attack.

On Wednesday afternoon the Turks attacked and about seven of them got into our trench. A German officer put his head over the trench and made a slash at a sergeant, who ducked and the sword just cut his cap. The sergeant drove his bayonet into the Hun, and he fell into our trench.

We then shipped our gun further up, and as there was no pit we fixed it on top of the trench. I started firing at the Turks who were 70 yards away, and after firing three rounds and the gun had been hit several times and its foresight knocked off, I was struck by a bullet on three fingers of the left hand, cutting a portion of one finger and injuring two others. My mate and I dismantled the gun and threw it into the trench. My wound was dressed by the sergeant, and I sat there for a couple of hours and had a smoke.

On the way to the beach, shells were dropping thickly, one of which exploded close behind me, and I was struck at the back of the knee and thrown into a watercourse. I was then carried to the beach on a stretcher. When I arrived at the dressing-station, I was given a drink of hot Bovril.

There were several hundred wounded men there, waiting to be taken aboard the transports. The sides of the hills were honeycombed with dugouts for the wounded. During the short time I was in the trenches, piers had been erected, two wireless stations erected on the beach, and there were piles of munitions, stores etc. on the beach. The wireless stations keep in touch with the sea-planes which have been flying overhead (to observe the enemy) since we landed.

I was put on board the hospital ship about 1 p.m. where there were about 850 wounded. Forty-seven died from their wounds on the voyage to Alexandria. I was sent to Heliopolis hospital. Septic poisoning set in my wound and put me back a few weeks; but the fresh air on the voyage home to Australia put me right.

Before leaving Egypt I reported for duty, but was considered unfit for service and thus was invalided home. We got a splendid reception at Adelaide and Melbourne, and, as early as possible, every man was given a month's leave with pay."

Signaller Charles M. Alexander writes this full and descriptive letter to his parents at St. Arnaud. This is one of the longest letters in the collection and is full of the "Anzac Spirit".

Convalescent Home,
Ras-El-Tin,
Egypt.
24th. July, 1915.

Dear Mother.

"1 have been slightly wounded. I was standing outside our dug-out when a bullet struck me just above the right knee, and penetrated the fleshy part of my leg. It is nothing serious, and save for the mark it is absolutely well. I have been having a great spell in the hospital for a few weeks. In a few days I hope to be back on the old Peninsula.

On the day of the landing I was detailed for duty, unloading stores, so I was a spectator of the sublime scene.

After a voyage from Lemnos Island, our transports assembled off the mist-shrouded shore of the Gallipoli Peninsula, and at dawn our warships opened fire, with Turkish batteries spitting venomously in return.

The men of the Third Brigade pulled off from their transports in boatloads. They did not wait to reach dry land, but leaped into the water, holding their rifles up to keep them dry. Once on the land they divested themselves of their packs, formed a rough line, and charged up the first heights with the bayonet.

Their cheers, sounding across the water, told of our first success. Shortly afterwards my brigade embarked in the boats and moved off towards the shore to reinforce them. Soon, rifle and machine-gun fire burst out violently, and a fierce struggle began.

After a while we were told that our men were chasing the Turks inland. The operations were carried out successfully, although at a tremendous cost. Before the sun set on that famous day, the same transports that brought us were packed with the wounded, and many a hero was dead.

I went ashore the next day and was pleased to discover that our company had suffered lightly in comparison with others. A firing-line had been hastily constructed the night before, and our troops were on the defensive. We were prepared to hold out to the last man!

God must have assisted us because the moonlight nights were our salvation. Our solitary battery nightly swept our Front with fire. Machine-guns rattled and rifles cracked their chorus of death. Then everything would cease and we re-filled our magazines and waited for the next movement. How we welcomed the dawn!

After a time, we were relieved from the trenches; and after a short rest we were greatly surprised to learn that our 2nd. Infantry Brigade had been ordered to Cape Helles (at the foot of the Peninsula) to show the Tommies how to fight!

Well, we travelled down to the Point on one of the naval destroyers. The English "bluejackets" are a splendid body of men. They supplied us with hot cocoa, which kindness we greatly appreciated, as the night was bitterly cold. We reached our destination in safety, and disembarked.

The country there is very different from that at Gaba Tepe because it has been under cultivation. It is flat country and the fields were bright with flowers when we arrived — mostly daisies and poppies. We marched past the ruined shore defences, and the remains of the town of Sedd-el-Bahr. It reminded me of the ruined cities of Italy. It looked as if it had been devastated by a violent earthquake, so completely had our Navy done its work.

French, British and Senegalese are operating there, so we had an opportunity of watching them at work. The enemy had been driven back about five or six miles, and the Allied lines stretched across the Peninsula, from sea to sea.

We had a couple of days' rest and on the never-to-be-forgotten day of May 8th. our particular work commenced. In co-operation with New Zealand Infantry we were to have the honour of carrying the British lines forward on the left Front.

About 4 o'clock, as far as I can remember, our movement began. We proceeded cautiously along a deep winding river-bed, which here and there contained deep water-holes. It was literally "the Valley of Death". Here and there a terrible stench told of bodies hastily covered over. A blackened limb protruded from the soft sandy bed in places to confirm our suspicions. We were marching on top of the dead.

Turkish ammunition and clothing lay everywhere, telling of hasty flight. We were being subjected to severe artillery fire and many of our men were falling. Then the Allied artillery, supported by the fire from our battleships, made effective reply. The din was deafening.

Far to our Front the shells covered the skyline and the sky

was discoloured with smoke as the village of Krithia burst into flames.

From a short distance behind the most advanced British outpost, we emerged from the valley, and deploying in companies, commenced to move forward at the double. We were greeted with a perfect hail of rifle and machine-gun fire.

We leaped over the top of the English trenches shouting, "On Australians! On Australians!" The Tommies crouching in their earthworks could not believe their senses. "Look at them! Look at them!" they cried. The bullets fell around us like hailstones and it seemed impossible to escape.

Every few hundred yards we momentarily halted to regain our breath, then up again and at them! Officers and men were falling fast. Colonel Gartside was shot dead while leading his men forward, and the adjutant, Captain Possingham, was killed by a stray bullet after the advance began. The ground was strewn with our dead and wounded.

At last we could push on no further. Though greatly exhausted we began to dig in. We had advanced a thousand yards more than was expected from us. I reached the line, more dead than alive, with the sweat flowing from me, but with a feeling of great thankfulness for being still alive.

Somehow or other I managed to keep hold of a pick; which came in very useful as many others had dropped their entrenching tools in the excitement. We needed no inducement to work, and by nightfall had raised a substantial barrier of earth for protection.

We continued digging all night, some working while others watched, peering into the gloom; but except for a feeble fire at intervals we were not greatly molested.

The men of the different battalions were mixed up in hopeless confusion. It looked as if all the officers had been wiped out, but everyone knew his work and did his duty without needing orders.

Shortly after sunset our left joined up with the New Zealanders. They had advanced over the country on the other side of the river-bed. It was a night of horror, never to be forgotten by those who were there.

The groans and cries of the wounded who were exposed to the bitter cold rang out all through the night. We were successful, but at a terrible cost. Half of our men were dead or wounded, but fortunately the wounded far outnumbered the dead; most of them will rejoin their battalions in the future when they are patched up.

Under cover of darkness, numerous reinforcements arrived and established support trenches a little to our rear; so by dawn we had made our position secure.

Snipers abounded here (as at Gaba Tepe) because the country affords splendid concealment for them. The periscopes are a great boon by enabling the sentries to keep watch without exposing their heads. Constant vigilance is the price of security in trench warfare.

After remaining in our position for four days we were relieved by English soldiers. We then marched through the valley to the rear, where we enjoyed a well-earned rest. General Ian Hamilton (Commander-in-Chief) sent us a message of congratulation.

The "crack-shot" of our battalion in Sergeant Hal Young (now Lieutenant). He shot <u>eight</u> snipers — a very difficult achievement considering the manner in which the Turks manage to conceal themselves.

Arthur Summerfield was with me in the firing-line; and Walter McNicol and Alick Dunlop came through it alright.

We rested about a week and then returned to Gaba Tepe,

and for a while acted as supports to the firing-line. We were in support the morning of the great Turkish attack on May 19th.

At 3 o'clock in the morning the Turks advanced with their bayonets fixed. They had been heavily-reinforced with fresh troops from Constantinople, and had been ordered by their German Officers to drive us into the seat

Our men let them approach quite close, and then our machine-guns and rifle fire mowed them down in hundreds. Our men disdained to take cover. They sat straddle legs on the sand bags and clambered over the parapets to get a better aim,

The Turkish attempt to drive us into the sea failed. Their dead and wounded littered the ground in front of our trenches = they lay in their thousands. But they had shown the greatest bravery, many of them reaching our entanglements only to die. Our casualties were few in comparison.

After a few days it was almost impossible to remain in the trenches, so bad was the stench. The hot weather causes rapid decomposition and the smell was indescribable, but for all that we had to eat our food amidst it till an Armistice could be arranged; and those bodies were not buried until May 24th. (six days later).

The scenery here is beautiful. The hills are verdant with vegetation. Flowers bloom everywhere and deep valleys open out towards the sea. Across the bay lies the rugged island of Embros, veiled in purple mists which occasionally lift to reveal the contour of the land.

To the right the white sands of Cape Suvla gleam in the sunshine, and craft of all description (from mighty battleships to the tiny destroyers) dart over the water.

At present, our 2nd. Brigade is having a rest on the island

of Embros, but the wounded have been sent to Egypt. Suitable buildings have been fitted up at Cairo and Alexandria, and Egypt is full of wounded soldiers.

I am stopping at the convalescent home at Ras-El-Tin, near the Sultan's palace, and close to the spot where he was nearly assassinated. I have numerous friends here and enjoy myself greatly. They are very kind and whenever I visit them there is no restraint. We all sing and eat and talk.

People here mostly live in flats. I know a great deal of Arabic and can get on alright in conversation. I have just been to see a Coptic family and we drank coffee out of dainty little cups, no bigger than doll's cups.

When I told my friend's mother that I had left my mother and father to come to the war, she gave me a compassionate look and said, "Oamach maskein," which means, "Poor mother". I have received no letters lately but I suppose they have gone to the Dardanelles. I have sent you some views of Alexandria which I hope you will like."

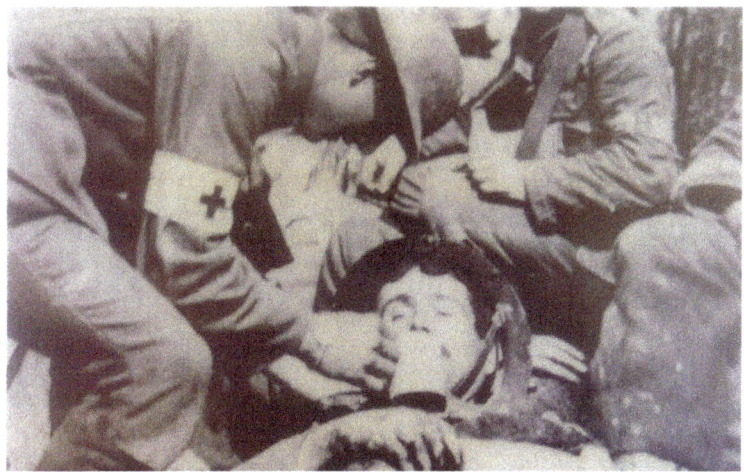

Angels Of Mercy

REMEMBERING 'LONE PINE' – AUGUST, 1915.

There is not doubt that after studying the history of Australia's wars surely its most famous battle took place in Gallipoli at a place called 'Lone Pine'. This fierce battle to capture Turkish trenches, began on the 6th. August when men of the 1st. Australian Brigade attacked from Anzac Cove, just 500 metres below the enemy trenches at 'Lone Pine' — this place was named by a single tree that grew there.

The Anzacs, regardless of heavy enemy fire, raced towards the Turkish trenches which were heavily fortified by fences and completely covered with heavy logs. The Anzacs fired through gaps in the roof, tore the logs apart, jumped into the trenches and then shot or bayoneted the Turks in hand-to-hand fighting.

Those brave Anzacs gained an advantage against all odds in that first line of Turkish trenches and with the help of reinforcements they took more trenches over the following days until they eventually occupied all the enemy trenches at 'Lone Pine'. On both sides the dead and wounded lay in the thousands. The Australians lost more than 2200 men in five days of fighting — the Turks lost almost 7000.

On the morning of the 9th, August, 1915, with a very small party, Captain Alfred SHOUT charged down a trench occupied by the enemy and personally threw four bombs among them, killing eight and driving away the rest. Later that day, he captured a further length of the enemy's trench and continued personally to bomb the enemy at close range under very heavy fire. Most soldiers throw only one bomb at a time, but Shout lit three bombs simultaneously in his charge against the enemy's front-line. This gallant officer successfully threw two lighted bombs at the Turks, but the third bomb exploded as it was leaving his hand and he was severely wounded, losing his right hand. It also destroyed his left eye, cut up his face and burnt his chest and legs — he died from those dreadful wounds.

Therefore, it is not surprising that Captain Alfred Shout was awarded a Victoria Cross at Lone Pine for killing eight Turks and capturing a heavily-defended enemy trench — but, six other soldiers also won Victoria Crosses during those five days of fighting at 'Lone Pine' for it was one of the most desperate and bloody engagements in Australia's history.

DEATH AT LONE PINE
— *from Australian war correspondent Charles Bean.*

The Australian Attack At Lone Pine, August 6, 1915

THE BRUTAL BATTLE OF LONE PINE (6th.-10th. AUGUST 1915)

There was hand-to-hand fighting for five days when the Australians assaulted enemy trenches which were protected by fences of barbed wire and had covered roofs made of heavy logs. Yet they captured those heavily-fortified Turkish trenches, thus advancing their front line — and winning seven Victoria Crosses while doing so.

The Australians lost more than 2200 men in five days of fighting — the Turks lost almost 7000.

A fierce battle to capture Turkish trenches had begun on the 6th. August when men of the 1st. Australian Brigade attacked from Anzac Cove, just 500 metres below Lone Pine (this place was named by a single tree that grew there). They reached the Turkish trenches which were heavily fortified by fences and with trench roofs made of heavy logs. The Anzacs fired through gaps in the roofs, tore the logs apart, jumped into the trenches and shot or bayoneted the Turks in hand-to-hand fighting.

HOW THESE SEVEN WON THEIR VICTORIA CROSSES
Private Leonard Maurice KEYSOR. VC
(A brave bomb-thrower who never stopped although wounded.)

Corporal William DUNSTAN, VC
(On 9 August 1915 at Lone Pine, Tubb, Burton and Dunstan succeeded in repulsing several enemy attacks on their trench and rebuilt the barricade.)

Lieutenant Frederick Harold TUBB. VC
(This officer, although wounded, and his two corporals — Dunston and Burton — several times repulsed the enemy and rebuilt the barricade of their newly-captured trench.)

Private John HAMILTON, VC
(On 9 August 1915 at Lone Pine, during a heavy attack by the enemy, Private Hamilton, bravely exposed himself on the parapet to obtain a better firing position against the enemy's bomb throwers.)

Captain Alfred John SHOUT. VC
(On 9 August 1915 at Lone Pine, Captain Shout led a small party down enemy trenches. He threw bombs and killed eight, and then continued to bomb the enemy at close range until he was wounded, losing his right hand and left eye. He died later from his injuries.)

Second Lieutenant William John SYMONS, VC
(Repelled several enemy attacks on his captured trench.)
Corporal Alexander Stewart BURTON. VC
(Killed while continually building up the trench parapet under a hail of bullets.

BATTLE OF LONE PINE

1. Leonard Keysor VC
2. William Dunstan VC
3. Frederick Tubb VC
4. John Hamilton VC
5. Alfred Shout VC
6. William Symons VC
7. Alexander Burton VC

DEATH AND GLORY AT LONE PINE
– WITH 2,000 DEAD AND 7 V.C'S.

THE BATTLE OF LONE PINE

Today, throughout Australia, one can find various memorials to our brave Anzacs — and sometimes one sees a huge pine tree, purported to have been grown from a seedling that has been brought here from Gallipoli. Such a tree is perhaps the most appropriate memorial for our soldiers, as it reminds us especially of "The Battle of Lone Pine". The plaque beneath such a tree tells us about that particular battle: -

AT 4-30 A.M. ON AUGUST 6, 1915, AN OFFICER BLEW A WHISTLE AND THE AUSTRALIANS CHARGED FROM THEIR TRENCHES INTO A CLOUD OF SHRAPNEL AND A TORRENT OF BULLETS. SOME FELL BEFORE THEY CLEARED THEIR PARAPETS, OTHERS WITHIN A FEW STRIDES,

LONE PINE WAS CAPTURED AND REINFORCED, BUT THE A.I.F. LOSSES WERE EXTREMELY HIGH, MORE THAN 2,000 AUSTRALIANS WERE KILLED OR

WOUNDED IN THIS SINGLE ENGAGEMENT, MOST OF
THEM IN HAND-TO-HAND FIGHTING HEAVIER THAN
ANY OTHER IN WHICH THE AUSTRALIANS WERE TO
TAKE PART THROUGHOUT THE GREAT WAR, OF THE
NINE VICTORIA CROSSES AWARDED TO AUSTRA-
LIANS ON GALLIPOLI, SEVEN WERE WON AT LONE
PINE.

WALLACE McILROY, of St. Arnaud, and his brother, **GEORGE
McILROY,** *were both fighting throughout the Gallipoli Campaign.
George was lucky and was not wounded; in fact, he had risen to be
second lieutenant with a remuneration of seven guineas per week.*

Wallace was in the greatest charge since the war began —
that of the Light Horsemen at Lone Pine which was said to
equal the famous charge of the Light Brigade in 1854 during
the Crimean War. In that charge a few men returned, but
the Eighth Light Horse at Lone Pine were nearly all to a man
wiped out.

Wallace was in a squadron of 150 and all, except two, were

either killed or wounded. Wallace's regiment comprised 600 men, divided into squadrons of 150 each. It was his regiment's duty to lead the charge so they drew lots to see which squadron would go first and in fell to the lot of Wallace's squadron to lead.

What with the roar of the big guns from the warships and the field artillery; the bursting of shells and bombs; the whistling of bullets — the noise was simply deafening. (But Wallace had always said he was not afraid to die for his country.)

As soon as they left the cover of their trenches the men began to drop like flies. Wallace was close to Colonel White when the latter fell with seven bullets through him. Then Wallace got hit with a flying piece of metal from a shell, but it just struck his haversack and lodged in a piece of bread. However, the force of the blow knocked him off his feet, but did him no serious harm. He also escaped three bullets which went through his shirt, but soon afterwards a bullet shattered his arm and brought him down.

He lay out there in No-Man's Land for several hours with bullets whistling over him and shells dropping and bursting around him. One bomb landed so close that it smashed his rifle to pieces, killed several of his comrades, but never did him any more harm than to stun him. He watched other men blown to pieces. When the smoke and dust cleared away, he looked around for his mates, but they were all down — it was several hours before Wallace could be rescued by a stretcher party.

<u>Private G. Guyatt</u> (of Donald) was wounded at Gallipoli — and his brother, Corporal Herbert Guyatt, was killed in action there after three months.

Malta Hospital.   <u>1915.</u>

LONESOME PINE

"I was on the Gallipoli Peninsula for ten weeks before the Turks got me. I stopped a bullet and a piece of shell in the wrist, and had a bayonet thrust into my leg. I have been under the X-Rays at the hospital here in Malta.

I saw poor Herb a few days before he was killed in action. It was Hell on earth that day. The Turks poured shell after shell into us, until the warships (firing from the bay) put a stop to their little game.

There has been a great battle in progress on the Peninsula these last few weeks, and several divisions of Tommies have been landed to assist us. <u>But the best fighter that ever wore a uniform is the Gurkha</u>: nothing can live when pitted against him.

The day I received my wounds there was a great battle fought. We attacked at 5-30 one evening, and carried four lines of trenches, and what trenches these were! The first line we came to was covered with great spars and shrubs; it was almost impossible to enter them. However, an entrance was made, and we bayoneted the Sultan's hopes from trench to trench.

But the Ottoman forces made a counter-attack with deadly hand bombs, and we gave them a good exchange. This lasted throughout the night; it was simply Hell let loose. We had dead Turks piled up high between the trenches. Their trench was only 10 yards from us."

(This brave Donald soldier took part in the attack upon strong Turkish positions along Lone Pine ridge. Here, Turkish trenches were like underground fortresses, roofed with pine logs and great beams of wood. On August 6th. — at 5.30 p.m. as Private Guyatt says — when the Australians reached these trenches, they had to cut their way in, exposed all the time to a withering fire from machine-guns and heavy artillery. Once inside the trenches, Australians came to handgrips with the Turks. They captured Lonesome Pine and also a crop of 7 Victoria Crosses. The Turkish counter-attacks lasted for 72 hours.)

DEATH AT LONE PINE

— from Australian war correspondent Charles Bean.

'The obstruction of all supplies was caused by the dead and wounded clogging the trenches.'

'His trench was filled two and three deep with dead and dying men — there was no barrier across the trench except the bodies of the dead.'

'Climbing the track they found themselves passing rows of Turkish dead laid out four deep — "a column of dead men".'

'The trench was literally floored with the dead, in places several deep, and so the fight had to be carried on over their bodies.'

'The dead lay so thick that the only respect which could be paid to them was to avoid treading upon their faces.'

'The men of the 1st. Brigade were not only completely exhausted, but also sick with the stench of the dead.'

Water tank at Gallipoli (7th. August, 1915) near Steele's Post. Photo — Gunner Geddie Pearse.

TROOPER 177. WILLIAM McELINNEY — 8th. LIGHT HORSE - killed in action on 7th. August, 1915, during the charge on Turk trenches at The Nek.

8th Light Horse recruits (from left) Llewllyn Weiss, of Windsor, William McElhinney, of Birchip, Bill Blackburn, of Alphington. Seated, Arthur Leeman, of Snake Valley.

GALLIPOLI: THE CHARGE OF THE 3RD. LIGHT HORSE BRIGADE

AT THF NEK — 7th. August, 1915

Oil painting by G. W. Lambert (Australian War Memorial)

Turkish Soldiers

The Battles of August

SLAUGHTER AT THE NEK

Never in history was any military campaign richer in acts of heroism and self-sacrifice; but there is no finer example of courage, obedience and mateship than that shown by the 8th. and 10th. Australian Light Horse Regiments during their charge against THE NEK.

It was the 7th. of August when our Light Horsemen were ordered to capture a narrow piece of land. However, during the previous night the Turks had secretly reinforced their trenches and, in fact, were lining their parapets with rifles and machine guns in readiness for any attack.

Trooper James Faulkner, described what happened at The Nek on his return home to Watchem at a "Welcome Back" ceremony.

Trooper Faulkner, was in that first line led by Lt-Colonel White, the officer whose body was torn and riddled by Turkish bullets before he had even gone ten paces. The first line of 150 Light Horsemen had started out so confidently, but were annihilated in half-a-minute

Then, lying wounded in No Man's land, Trooper Faulkner watched the second line of 150 Light Horsemen appear over the top of the parapet. But what chance did they have? These brave men were charging machine- guns and rifles in short sleeves and short pants and carrying only fixed bayonets.

That second line was led by Major Arthur Deeble — and the 150 Light Horsemen rushed forward into a hail of bullets, straight to their death — although Major Deeble somehow survived.

Immediately, a third line of 150 men suddenly appeared

over the parapet. They were the 10th. Light Horse Regiment from Western Australia — AND THEY, TOO, RAN FORWARD TO MEET DEATH INSTANTLY.

At that point a Turkish officer yelled out, *"No more! No more!"* because even the enemy was sickened by the senseless slaughter of such brave men.

In spite of everything that had gone before, then the fourth line went over the top.

Apparently, the brigadier was discussing withdrawal tactics when an officer waiting in the Australian trench misunderstood a signal and ordered the fourth line to proceed.

Can you imagine how those men felt? They knew that death was a certainty but they would not disobey for fear of letting down their mates.

"RELIABILITY, OBEDIENCE and MATESHIP" is their motto.

So, over the top went another 150 Light Horsemen to meet death instantly as every man ran as swift and as straight as he could towards the Turkish trenches — only to fail beneath the tempest of bullets.

¶

There's a story that Colonel Deeble threw a Turkish revolver into a dam on his Corack property in the 1930's. He had taken it from a dead Turk at The Nek. Why did he throw a Turkish souvenir away after 20 years? Perhaps it was a constant reminder of the terrible slaughter — or did he blame it for the drought which ruined his farming career?

¶

How The Wounded Were Conveyed To The Hospital Ships.

BATTLE OF THE NEK

Who is not horrified by the battle of the Nek at Gallipoli, in the early hours of August 7, 1915, when four waves of Australian soldiers (600 diggers) followed orders and charged straight at Turkish machineguns just 40 metres away, only to be cut down like young blades of wheat before death's swinging scythe.

Before the third wave of soldiers went out from their trench, the Turks themselves were shouting at the Australians, a strange pleading call, "Dur! Dur! Dur!" ("Stop! Stop! Stop! Do not keep running into our guns, slaughtering yourselves!")

Too late. In the space of mere minutes, no fewer than 372 of those Australian soldiers went down.

Let us never forget that the First World War took no less

than 16 million lives of all the nations involved. Australia sent 332,000 to serve overseas and of that number 61,000 never returned home.

The Battle of The Nek was one of the bravest charges in history. This ill-fated attack on the Nek at Gallipoli took place in the cold dawn of August 7th. in 1915. It was 4-30am and at the sound of a whistle out of the trenches poured young Anzacs of the 8th„ and 10th. Light Morse Regiments to he greeted by the waiting machine-guns of the Turkish defenders.

Australian Light Horsemen

Colonel Arthur DEEBLE

Colonel White led the first line of 150 Light-horse men over the top against a line of blazing Turkish machine-gun fire that cut through the bone and flesh of nearly every gallant trooper in that charge. Within about 30 seconds the first line wilted and faded away — many men fell backwards into the trench, dead or wounded, before even clearing the parapet. Colonel White barely ran ten paces before his body was torn and riddled by bullets.

Nobody tried to stop the second line as they jumped out to follow the courageous example of their fellow troopers. Major Deeble, in charge of the second line, bravely led his men over the parapet, and as they rose up, cheering, a terrible storm of bullets mowed them down like grass. So how did Major Deeble manage to survive? Because he saw the first line massacred and had the sense to lie still where he fell in the rush. After clearing the parapet Deeble spent the next hour or so hugging the ground with shrapnel falling like the rain around him.

SANGUINARY AUGUST

Trooper J. J. Faulkner (8th. Light Horse) the son-in-law of Mr. S. Skewes, returned home to Watchem in October, 1915, having been seriously wounded in the chest, right arm and hip. He speaks of his experiences in the 3rd. Light Horse Brigade at the Dardanelles.

"I was with Trooper Tierney (Watchem) and in the same company as Lieutenant Sproat (Donald). Two other comrades of mine were Trooper H. Grace (Birchip) and Trooper McElhinney (Birchip) — both of whom were killed on August 7th. during the storming of the Turkish trenches upon the Nek.

In Egypt, the 8th. Light Horse had undergone training with the bayonet — similar to the infantrymen — but beyond this, all our work had been with the horses. Therefore we were at a considerable disadvantage when orders came for us to embark for Gallipoli as infantrymen.

We received word on the Wednesday, and for the next two

days we had to march across the hot desert sands. On the following Saturday we embarked for the Firing-line.

We landed at Anzac on May 19th. — about three weeks after the memorable arrival of the Australians on Gallipoli. Our 3rd. Brigade included the 8th. 9th. and 10th. Light Horse Regiments. When we arrived, a big engagement had just about finished.

The Turks had attacked the Australian trenches and been repulsed with a loss of about 7,000 men. {This was the Great Turkish Assault of May 19th.}

Well, we went into the trenches and began the usual routine of an Australian soldier's life on Gallipoli. We might go two or three days without firing a rifle, and then there would be a bit of an affray.

In one attack the Turks had between 500 and 600 killed and they were lying close to our trenches; so the bodies lying close to our parapets were sprayed with paraffin and burnt, but others further out had to stay where they were. The Turks asked us for an Armistice to bury the dead, but their request was refused as the previous Armistice (on May 24th.) had been violated. Instead of just burying their dead, the Turks had sneakily brought up stores and shifted guns etc. during the lull in the fighting.

Apart from that one incident, as far as I can see, the Turks always fought fairly.

We had rather a slack time in the trenches until <u>August 7th</u>. We were, given two or three days' notice of a big attack for that day and we were instructed to prepare for it. After eleven weeks of trench-digging and water-carrying we were all eager to attack the enemy and push them back into the open country.

Orders were given that we had to pack up our blankets

and overcoats and leave them at the Quarter-master's store. For some strange reason our tunics were taken away and we were left practically without clothes, except for our shirts, short pants and puttees.

We were told to attack in short sleeves, without cartridges, relying solely upon the bayonet.

We waited all Thursday night (August 4th.) anticipating the order to attack; but it did not come until about 3 o'clock on Saturday morning. I can tell you, those nights were cold without our tunics and we had little sleep.

An intense bombardment by warships, destroyers and land artillery gave us an indication that the time was at hand. We waited in two lines in the front trenches on Russell's Top. The men of the 8th. began to prepare to leap from the trenches by pulling down sandbags to stand on.

The job before us was known to be a tough one, as this spot was known as the "Chessboard" — owing to the number of moves and counter-moves and changes there in the early part of the landing, and was recognised as one of the most difficult places to attack.

Just before the first peep of day (about 4-30 a.m.) the bombardment began to slacken and Lieutenant-Colonel White (Commanding Officer of the 8th.) looked at his watch. He passed the word along. "Five minutes to go," then, "Three minutes to go," and then, "Get ready," and finally, "Jump parapet!"

His orders followed in quick succession. In an instant our first line eagerly leapt over the parapet. Not a stone's throw away were the trenches of the enemy, and as soon as our heads appeared above, the Turks opened fire with machine-guns and rifles.

Many of our boys were shot and fell back into the

trenches, wounded before even clearing the parapet. Young McElhinney (of Birchip) was one of these. The rest of us dashed forward as hard as we could go with fixed bayonets.

It was like running into a hailstorm and it was not a matter of wondering if I would get hit, but where I would be hit.

I saw Colonel White fall — and practically all the rest. I had gone a few yards when I was struck slightly on the hip — it was like a burn. Then a second bullet went through my chest and at the same time another bullet struck me on the right shoulder.

The sensation was as if I had been struck with a brick, or as if a horse had kicked me. There was no pain at first, but just a numb sensation. I fell and lay for some time in a depression in the ground.

I saw our second line of men leap forward into the tempest and then wilt away before that terrible hail of lead. The third line, made up of the 10th Light Horse, fared no better — running forward to meet death instantly. One of their sergeants was the only man to actually reach the Turkish trench and he jumped straight in, and fought and died like a hero!

I was very lucky because when the Turkish fire was diverted, I seized the opportunity to crawl away and get over the crest of the ridge. Here I was fortunate enough to meet a mate who carried me to safety. This man had been struck in the left hand, and after getting it dressed he went back to see if he could help the wounded on the field. He assisted another man in, under heavy fire, and I think he deserved the V.C. medal.

When I arrived at the Dressing-Station on a stretcher, it was a strange coincidence that the Roll was being called and my name was called out just as I was being carried past; so I promptly replied, "Present."

And what a Roll-Call! Out of 530 stalwart and brave Australians who participated in the charge of the Nek on August 7th. only 47 answered the call, and most of these were leaning upon their comrades.

Seventeen officers were in that charge, twelve were killed outright, three severely wounded and only two were unhurt."

TROOPER JAMES ALFRED ANDERSON

James was born on the 31st. May, 1889, the son of Alexander Anderson, a farmer, and his wife, Margaret Hart. He enlisted at Rupanyup on the 16th. September, 1914, and joined the 8th. Light Horse Regiment. This excellent horseman and intelligent soldier was soon promoted to Lance-Corporal.

Now, although the Light Horse Brigades had been trained in Egypt to fight on horseback against the Turks in the desert, by June (1915) it was considered necessary to ship some of Australia's mounted troops to Gallipoli to strengthen the infantry regiments there which had lost so many men. Consequently, these magnificent soldiers had to leave behind their faithful horses in Egypt to go and fight on the Turkish hillsides in .Gallipoli — and amongst those untrained "infantrymen" was Trooper James Anderson.

At first the newly-arrived light-horsemen experienced unfamiliar trench-warfare, involving several weeks of trench-digging and water-carrying; but by August they were ready to take part in a vitally important assault upon a Turkish position. At the beginning of August it was decided that the actual storming of the Nek would be made by the 3rd. Light Horse Brigade. This gigantic task was confidently anticipated by the light-horse staff who did not think the Turkish trenches would be so heavily manned.

The two regiments chosen for this assault were the 8th. (Victorian) and the 10th. (Western Australia) and there would be four lines (two from each regiment) who would leave their trenches in quick succession. In theory the idea was a good one — i.e. the first line would seize the Turkish trenches on the Nek; the second line would pass over and capture the enemy trenches on Baby 700; the third line would capture the trenches further behind; and the fourth line would carry picks and shovels to dig new trenches as required.

It was stated in their orders that attacking troops would have full support from naval guns on the warships and also from nearby mountain guns and howitzers. (Trooper Faulkner's letter describes how their tunics were taken away and how they shivered in the deep trenches for two bitterly-cold nights while awaiting the signal to attack.)

The 8th. Light Horsemen were in position at the front trench which was a deep one with pegs driven into the wall for the men to hold onto — and with niches cut out for their feet — so that when the signal came to attack they would be able to spring out of the trench in a flash. Their popular commander, Lt.-Colonel A. H. White, was to lead the attack (and he would have known full well that he could never survive). Behind them were men of the 10th. ready to take their place as soon as the two lines of the 8th had gone forward

No one knows why the supporting guns stopped firing before the attacking time of 4-30 a.m. but they did and this pause in the firing allowed the enemy time to enter their trenches; prepare their machine-guns along the parapets; and put rifles to their shoulders in readiness.

Trooper Anderson died in that attack on the Nek (7th. August), but was he in that first line which leapt over the top with such eagerness? Those first men did not know they would be mown down within half-a-minute; however, the second line of soldiers would know exactly what fate awaited them from those deadly machine-guns facing them less than a stone's throw away.

L/Cpl. JAMES ALFRED ANDERSON
- 8th,. Light Horse Regiment

Private Ged Pearse, of Donald, writes home to his parents.

GABA TEPE,
10th. August, 1915

Dear Mother,

We have been through Hell, and how we are still alive beats me! There has been a very big move on here, and the Tommies are doing great work. No doubt you will have read about it in the papers, ere you receive this.

Poor old Bert Glasson was killed, and Reg. Shallberg, who is a second lieutenant, was put out of action when his fingers were blown off and his leg badly damaged. I believe that Jack D'Arcy has been sent away with shellshock and he does look a wreck. Bert Box was wounded some time ago. However, all the other lads from Donald are doing well.

What little bombardment the Turks gave us played up with our nerves; but we bombarded the Turks about 20 times as heavily, so what must their nerves be like?

I know that over 700 Turkish prisoners have been captured so far; and the way our field guns and the gun boats are still blazing away at them there can't be many of them left.

I can't tell you any of our movements as secrecy is the main thing in war. I hope that our next big move will mean the finish of this part of the war, for I have no desire to see any more. It is simply an endless slaughtering of human beings.

It is terrible the way those big shells play up with our nerves so that we even duck at our own shells. One takes no notice of the shrapnel shells. It's the 6 inch high explosives that do the damage.

The Turks were only firing one or two big guns, the biggest being 9.2 inch; while we have been shelling them with anything from our field guns (18 pounders) to the 14 inch on the gunboats. It is a beautiful sight to see a bombardment — although it is not nice to be in one.

I have read in the "Argus" letters from our wounded soldiers and they state that the Turks are cowardly fighters, and that they use explosive bullets. I really must deny this.

It is now 24 hours later and we are in a better position — away from the shells.

One of the gun crews came and relieved us so that our nerves will have a bit of a rest. The trenches here are splendid and not knocked about. Things are very quiet today · the first time since this big move took place.

Five days is a long time without rest so I feel better today after a good night's sleep. It is hoped that we are getting near the end of all this business, as the sooner alt is over, the better for the rest of the world.

We have just heard that there is a mail in and I hope it is true, for a mail does more to put one in good spirits than anything else I know.

The day the big move started, I never saw such a crowd of boats. Hospital ships, gunboats, transports, destroyers and tugs for miles over the sea.

At this moment our aeroplanes are having a look round to find out what the Turks are doing. Planes play a great part in this game, and they save us from a great many surprise attacks. Two of our planes attacked a German Taube last night and it was great fun watching them.

All our boys wish to be remembered to all our friends at home. It is very warm today — perhaps it is because we have time to feel the sunshine.

We have just been told that Germany wants peace with Russia. Well, I have seen some terrible sights since the last bombardment started, and that also helps to break one up.

We had a jolly time with a big bunch of letters from our dear home folk. I received a parcel from a kind English lady called Mrs. Boswell (of Wolverhampton) containing a cake, three cigars, two packets of cigarettes and some chocolate.

I did not have it for more than five minutes before the end came. All the boys had to have a taste — of course, George ate half the parcel — for "what's one's belongs to the other".

Sixteen men were buried yesterday by a high explosive shell. I believe they were all killed. Weeks here fly like days to me, and the only consolation is that every day that passes is a day longer that I have lived and a day nearer home." { The day after writing these lines Ged Pearse received a bullet wound in his arm. }

HUGO VIVIAN HOPE THROSSELL, V. C. (1884-1933)

Hugo Vivian Hope Throssell is famous as the first Victoria Cross winner from Western Australia. With the outbreak of war in 1914, he and a brother joined the Light Horse Regiment and were sent to train in Egypt. But when there was a shortage of infantrymen in Gallipoli, the Light Horse Regiment had to leave their horses in Egypt and go to help. Lieutenant Throssell arrived there just in time to take part in that suicidal charge at the Nek on August 7th. He was in the fourth and last line of troops which survived because they were called back from the attack just in time to avoid more senseless slaughter.

Perhaps to compensate for surviving at the Nek where so many other Light Horsemen were killed, Throssell eagerly led his men of the 10th. Light Horse on the 29th. August to capture a Turkish trench at Hill 60. It was a fierce fight with both sides throwing more than 3000 bombs at each other across the sandbags. The Western Australians were picking up the bombs and hurling them back at the Turks and although the enemy made three rushes at the Australian trench, they were driven back by showers of bombs and rifle-fire.

Thossell was wounded twice and his face was covered with blood from bomb splinters; yet he repeatedly yelled encouragement to his men and led them forward until the Turks retreated. For his part in that fierce battle Hugo Throssell was awarded the Victoria Cross.

In 1920 Hugo married the Australian writer, Katherine Pritchard, and they had a son. Yet on 19th. November, 1933, this brave Victoria Cross soldier shot himself. He had lost his job and was in debt — and suffering from severe depression in spite of having won the highest medal for valour. His wife, who dearly loved him, was then left alone to care for their son.

*Captain Hugo Throssell was awarded
the VC for his bravery at Gallipoli.*

Two Donald brothers, ALBERT and RICHARD ALLAN, were both fighting at Gallipoli. In the following letter (dated September 4th. 1915, from a Maltese hospital) Albert says he has a bad back incurred through sleeping in wet clothes and he describes some of his experiences.

"On August 9th. We were prepared to move on and by dawn we were on a flat near a large salt lake to the left of the enemy. When the Turks became aware that we were there, they opened fire on us and we at once replied. The lead, like hail, began to fly everywhere and I was expecting to get hit at any moment. We forced our way up the hill and made the Turks worried, but it was murder to be there. Naturally, we were very glad when darkness descended.

Some 'Tommies' were sent to relieve us and then we dug

ourselves in. When the English soldiers arrived they had to dig a trench and so we then had a rest at the bottom of the hill. On Sunday morning the order came that at daybreak we were to go out an draw fire from the Turks on Hill 971 while the English stormed another position. We went out in fine style and it was here that I counted myself lost because when we reached the top of the hill I was level with the skyline and the Turks began to shoot at me.

One bullet broke the stock of my rifle and after I procured another rifle they smashed the butt of that one. I had the luck to find another rifle and then ran like a hare. We were only 200 yards from the Turkish trenches and they opened fire on us with machine guns, shrapnel and rifle. The fire was awful and it was Hell to be there. The 'Tommies' were advancing to the rear of the Turks, whilst about 600 yards away Turkish reinforcements could be seen coming. When the Allied Fleet noticed this they put a shell into them and pieces of Johnny Turk could be seen flying everywhere.

When the navy lobs a shell into their trench the Turks go up in the air — perhaps a head, leg, or an arm. It is an awful death. It was in this charge that we lost poor Jim Booley, of Donald. He was put down as missing in action. I shall never forget that Sunday as long as I live. When coming back we passed dead Turks lying everywhere. Later on I was ordered out on outpost duty and sniping It was on that night that we lost poor Joe Hoare. He had been out sniping and was just returning to the line when the moon began to shine and the Turks detected him and wounded him very badly.

We had seven charges in less than two weeks. On August 21st we fixed bayonets and as soon as the navy had finished a bombardment we had to charge. The Turks tried to stop us, but when they see our cold steel they duck for their lives. A few of us went over the hill, but were ordered to come back. On the top of the hill I slipped and rolled down to the bottom. I knew if I moved they would shoot me. However, I noticed a hole in the ground and so got in it, just in time, for the Turks let me have a volley or two, but missed.

I noticed one poor fellow who was wounded badly, but he moved and the Turks fired on him. Poor chap, the Turks soon got him and many other wounded heroes with him. It was cruel to see them being murdered. We could not secure any bodies until the darkness came and when the stretcher-bearers came for me they noticed these poor fellows and exclaimed, "Good God, they have shot the wounded!"

It was on this night that we lost our parson, one of the best fellows possible. He was attending the wounded when a sniper shot him in the chest and the poor fellow died in a few minutes. Next morning I was on the hospital ship. Such is the fortune of war!"

Pte. Richard Allan
and
his two sons

*In a London Military Hospital Pte. George Wardlty,
seated at the front left with dog*

PRIVATE C. W. SCHULTZE *of St. Arnaud, writes from Anzac,
Dardanelles, to his mother, in a letter dated 16th. September, 1915.*

"We landed here on 7th. September in the dark and went into the trenches next morning. The Australians have done good work here. It seems strange being constantly under fire, but you soon get used to it. The Turks are only about 10 or 30 yards from us, so we can throw bombs by hand into their trenches.

The Turks are very fair fighters and it is a pity that the Germans do not take a lesson from them. There are flying machines over us at the present time, so our guns and rifles are firing for all they are worth, but it seems strange to see our men walking about as if nothing were going on.

This is a champion place for flies, and water is very scarce. I have not had a wash since I came here, and do not see any prospects of getting one. I am in good health and have so far escaped the shells, bullets and bombs. Several men, who came over on the same boat as I did from Australia, have been wounded and killed.

We are having splendid weather at present, but I believe it is very cold and wet here in the winter. We are living in holes, just like rabbits, on the side of the hills. I have had some very narrow shaves, though we do most of our fighting at night-time whilst the artillerymen work hard in the day-time. We are fed here better than I was in the South African war, but our drinking water is very scarce and we only get half a bottle a day, besides tea in the morning and evening.

The bullets are flying about three feet above my head at present, but of course I have sand-bags in front of me. I would just have to put my head up for a few seconds and that would be the end of me. We can see the Turks through our periscope and they are watching us the same way. That is in the day-time, but at night we put our heads over the parapet and take our chance.

In one trench opposite us the Turks had a good sniper, so good that one day he broke three periscopes in less than a minute. Yesterday, while looking through a loop-hole, I saw him exposing himself, so I fired a shot. I looked again and found he had put up two sandbags to hide behind. Then he showed his head for about half a second and I fired — he has not been seen since."

INFANTRY OF THE FRENCH ARMY.

Private Stanley Mole writes to his mother from a soldiers' convalescent home, on the 19th. September, 1915,

"I am now at a convalescent home for wounded soldiers. There are about 5,000 men here in this large hotel situated on the banks of the River Nile, about 20 miles from Cairo. Nearby are the large compunds where they keep all the Turkish prisoners we have captured at Gallipoli.

I still have a small wound in my shoulder, but it will soon heal up. I suppose you have read all about the battle that I got wounded in? It was at a place they call "The Lonesome Pine".

This battle started on Friday night, 6th. August, and it was still going strong when I got wounded on the following Monday morning, but our boys held on to those trenches like glue.

It was an awful sight when I came out of the battle. Our dead men were lying in the bottom of the trenches and I had to walk over their bodies — about a hundred of them — and when I reached the Dressing- Station the sight there was even worse.

The wounded covered every inch of the ground, waiting for the doctor to attend to them. There were only four Dressing-Stations on the beach and when I arrived I could see nothing but wounded soldiers. I never thought we had so many men at the Front.

We were put into a boat and taken out to a hospital ship — there were eight of these lying at anchor just off the beach. When we were safe on board a nurse gave us a large slice of bread and butter and a cup of cocoa. I thought I had never tasted anything so delicious in all my life.

We were all very hungry and thirsty, so we kept the nurses going with the cocoa and bread and butter for quite a while. Then an Indian doctor came and dressed my wound. We were then put on a minesweeper which carried us to the island of Udros and from there a bigger boat carried us to Egypt."

GALLIPOLI VETERANS
8th. Battalion
GABA TEPE
CAPE HELLES
KRITHIA
ACHI BABA
LONE PINE
HILL 971
SUVLA BAY
ANZAC BEACH
THE NEK
SARI BAIR
HILL 60
CHUNUK BAIR
QUINN'S POST
CHESSBOARD

SOMEONE'S CARELESSNESS

Private Georae Tierney (24th. Battalion) writes to his mother, Mrs. W. Fletcher, of St. Arnaud. Private Tierney is at Gallipoli with two of his brothers — Arthur and Bert.

Gallipoli. 21st. September. 1915.
"We landed here on Sunday, 6th. September, and had a couple of days' rest before going into the trenches. We were in the trenches for 48 hours and then out of them for 48 hours. We were glad to get out, as we had no sleep while in the trenches.

Do you know, I was in the trench for two days and all that time I was only 50 yards from brother Arthur's trench! One night I heard talking and recognised his voice. He had such a surprise to see me, that he hardly knew me at first. He was going to take me to see brother Bert, but next morning my Company was shifted away to a different trench. Then Arthur moved away on the following Friday for a rest, so I have not seen him since.

But the next day I met an old friend of Bert's who told me where Bert was entrenched, so I am going to try and find him. Anyway, the morning after I met Arthur, I saw Captain Duggan (of St. Arnaud) going to the Front with his men; and I told him where Arthur was and he went straight in to see him.

You'll be pleased to hear, Mother, that Arthur was not wounded at all; they got him mixed up with A. J. Tierney from Birchip!

When we are out of the trenches we live in a hole, just like rabbits. We get well-fed, and an issue of rum every day, and plenty of cigarettes — so we are not doing too badly. It is getting very cold here now winter is coming. Our Colonel asked us if we would like another blanket each. We said we would, so he put in a requisition for more. The Colonel is a fine fellow and the very picture of a soldier. Colonel Watson is his name.

Did you hear that the 21st. Battalion was torpedoed coming across from Egypt? In the confusion, their Brigadier lost his life. They were on the SOUTHLAND, and we were only about an hour's sailing in front of them. Each battalion came here on a separate boat.

Well, at first I shared a dug-out with Corporal Boyett and Corporal Usher; but Usher got a transfer to the machine-gun section, and the same day he and two others were killed by shrapnel. We have not had many casualties in my Company. But a very sad thing happened recently, right in front of my eyes.

It happened one day when we should have been relieved from the trenches at 8 o'clock — but the relieving battalion did not arrive until 11 o'clock. About a quarter-to-eleven, one of our fellows was going to throw a bomb over into the nearby Turkish trench and so he put the bomb on the ground to light it — instead of holding it in his hand. (The bomb goes off in five seconds after being lit.} After lighting it, he must have got too nervous and frightened to pick it up. One of our Corporals rushed forward to get it and throw it out of our trench — but it was too late«

The bomb went off in the brave fellow's hand. It blew his hand off, shattered his arm, and blew away his side. He died almost immediately. Two other men in the trench were killed, and two badly-wounded. Bert Farish {of St. Arnaud} was one of the wounded, but today I heard that he has since died. A thing like that, happening through someone's carelessness, is enough to break us up."

The Southland, shortly after being torpedoed

WILLIAM WHITE
– A FORGOTTEN SOLDIER

When a shell falls into a crowded trench and explodes, pieces of heads, legs and arms fly up into the air and then fall to the ground. It is an awful death — and during the constant walking of soldiers in and out of the Front-Line trenches those tiny human remains are trampled into the mud and soon disappear for ever.

One soldier killed in this tragic way was Private William White who therefore has no known grave and is forgotten. William (born in Bairnsdale on 20th. June, 1890) left home as a young man to find work around the country. He was a skilful sawyer so he eventually found employment on a property in the Wimmera. He lived in a hut on the owner's land and had all his meals supplied, although the wages were just a pittance. In the evenings he trained with the local Victorian Rangers which gave him good practice for a real war.

Soon William became friendly with a local farmer's pretty daughter. However, there is a class distinction that separates a landowner's daughter from a farm labourer, so when the farmer found out that they were friends he was furious and forbade his daughter to see William again.

When war began and perhaps keen to see the world, William volunteered immediately and enlisted at Broadmeadows on the 20th. August, 1914, at the age of 24.

He embarked on HMAT "Benalla" which was the first of sixteen transport ships that left Victoria between the 17th. and 21st. of October, bound for Egypt. Thus, Private William White was amongst the very first of about 330,000 AIF soldiers who embarked from Australia for overseas service. Not only were Australians the only volunteer soliders of any army involved in that First World War, but they also received the highest pay (6 shillings per day for a private) whilst the conscripted British soldier only received 'a bob a day'.

In Egypt, he trained at Mena Camp upon the desert sands in the shadow of the famous Pyramids and then went with his 8th. Battalion to Serapeum, helping to guard the Suez Canal from dangerous Turkish attacks.

In 1915 he landed with the 2nd. Infantry Brigade at Anzac Cove on Sunday, 25th. April, where they had to climb steep, rugged cliffs and drive back the Turks with only their bayonets. William bravely fought for the next few months on the Gallipoli Peninsula where 8,000 Anzacs were killed yet he survived those terrible battles.

William wrote at every spare moment to the farmer's daughter, although their letters were kept secret from her father.

He tells her, *"It is a terrible thing to be in a bayonet charge — it is hard to stick a man with a bayonet, but we got to fight for our lives and we are the boys to deal with the Turks. We Australians will never lose our good name — we will go through Hell. I am prepared to lay my life down for my King and Country at any time.*"

When winter arrived on the Peninsula and heavy rains drowned a few soldiers in the flooded trenches, William wrote to say that he had pneumonia and was being nursed in an Egyptian convalescent hospital.

In his next letter William tells his friend he had rejoined his battalion and had been transferred to the 2nd. Machine Gun Company; he says, "*My nerves have gone to pot lately due to the big gun-fire, but I suppose I will get over it in time. Anyhow, I am not afraid to die for my country. I am never going to leave this firing-line — I am going to see this war to the finish. We have to fight for every inch of ground we take and then carry it through with the point of our bayonets.*"

THE LOSS OF THE 'ROYAL EDWARD'- 18/8/15

{<u>Gunner Harold Beckham</u>, son of Mr. and Mrs, Beckham of Charlton Road, Donald, writes the following letter from ANZAC COVE to his parents, giving an eyewitness account of the sinking of a troopship by German U-Boats.}

<u>October. 1915.</u>
"I am in the pink of condition and safe in God's hands still. The Government may shortly want Dad to come over here as a sapper — to blast rocks and blow up tunnels — as Dad says he is now doing that kind of work on Mr. Sproat's farm.

When coming over from Alexandria to Lemnos Isle, I saw a dreadful sight. It was the torpedoing of H.M.S. ROYAL EDWARD, in the Aegean Sea. I was standing on the deck of the 'Alnwick Castle', not far behind that unfortunate ship.

We were steaming along very peacefully, when suddenly a great column of water shot up into the air, as high as the masthead of the ROYAL EDWARD. Then she slowly got lower astern, and we saw her bows rise up in the air until the ship was perpendicular. She then vanished within a few minutes, leaving only a cloud of smoke from her funnels to mark where she went down.

I do not think there was a man on board my ship who was not in a state of terror. The order came, "Below to your life-belts," and we got to them in double-quick time. It was not the time for slow movement, as the ROYAL EDWARD had disappeared within six minutes of being hit.

Our ship's speed was 15 knots, but she managed to do 17 knots that day because the German submarine wanted to sink us, too. We wore our life-belts all the following days and nights; and at night, in our fancy, we seemed to hear explosions and feel the ship shudder as if she were going down.

Oh, the horrors of it all, as we watched those soldiers go down with their ship. They had no time to get up on deck from down below. When I was on submarine guard the next night, every little sound made me feel as if cold water was being poured over me and I was drowning with them. Oh, I had the creeps, sure enough.

As long as I live, I never want to see another ship sink. Out of her 1,600 officers and troops, only 600 were saved. The ROYAL EDWARD was formerly known as H.M.S. CAIRO."

A TURKISH INFANTRYMAN

An Australian Light Horseman

Private O. Cain (14th. Battalion) returned home to Birchip as a wounded soldier, in October, 1915.

Dear Mother,

I am thinking of you all at home, so I will tell you a little about what has happened to us. On the 8th. August I noticed the following incident. There was a call for non-commissioned officers to lead a platoon to save a position from the Turks.

Sergeant Neyland (a Mallee farmer from Birchip) of B Company, at once sprang forward and volunteered his services. He led the platoon with great gallantry until eventually he fell into the hands of the Turks and was taken prisoner.

Some days later on the 21st. August, we were again in action — and while mounting a ridge one of my chums, Private Claude James, was shot down by the Turks and fell at my feet. He was already dead when I looked down, but there was a smile on his face. As far as I could ascertain he has no relatives alive, except a sister somewhere in Australia, who, if she only knew, would be proud of the way in which her brother died.

I saw another man in my company killed on the same day. His name was Mulany and his relatives will be glad to know that he died bravely and was killed so quickly that he did not suffer much pain.

Another observation about the 8th. August says much about discipline in the Australian regiments. We had to pass in single file, at the double, through the thick scrub upon which was concentrated the fire of about forty machine-guns belonging to the Turks. I tell you, the men of the 14th. Battalion exhibited a cool steadiness which upheld the best traditions of the British army.

There was no rushing or confusion, although men were

falling all around us. They just kept running at the double until they had gained their objective. When we looked behind we could see long lines of bodies, showing where the enemy fire had cut right through us."

A
Soldier
of the
A. I. F.

***Captain B. Duaaan** writes from Gallipoli to his father, Councillor Duggan, of Sutherland. He describes conditions in the trenches.*

<u>12th. November, 1915.</u>
"At last we have reached the firing-line. I'm writing this in my dugout, by the light of a slush-lamp (a tobacco tin, filled with fat and a wick in it).

The noise overhead is something terrible at times. Everything will seem to be at rest, when suddenly some of the big guns on the ships will open up — and talk about noise, it is enough to deafen one.

This morning was the loudest and biggest noise since we came here. One shell landed within 20 yards of our back sheds. They did rock it in.

You can look over the parapet of your trench with the aid of a periscope and not see any movement; but if you put your head up for a few seconds, you are lucky if you don't get a hole in it.

As far inland as we can see, there are Turkish trenches, so it's going to be a long, weary way to Constantinople.

The Autumn weather here is "bonzar". I'd be alright, only for being rooked (*robbed*) of all my clothing on board the SOUTHLAND when she was struck. Every second day here I have a shave, and then with the same water. I clean my teeth and wash my face. Sometimes it is a cupful, but sometimes it is less. About every second time, I get enough to wash my ears and neck. All the water is brought over from Alexandria, and, as something went wrong with the water-ship, we are now on half-rations.

The water is carried in cans for about half a mile from the beach, also our food rations. It is very hard work for the men. At first, the men in my company were a bit nervy, but now they are fit for anything.

In one enemy trench close to us, the Turks had a sniper who was so good that the day we arrived he broke three of our periscopes in less than a minute. So yesterday, while looking through a loophole, I saw him put up his head for a second, so I got a rifle and had a couple of shots at him, but only frightened him.

The Loss Of The "Aboukir," " Hogue," And "Cressy"

THE EVACUATTON

by Sergeant Alexander Walder of Watchem

After spending a fortnight on Anzac after my return from Lemnos Island, word began to get around that we were to be shifted from Gallipoli to some unknown destination. Now began the rumours as to when, and where, and how, we would be leaving Anzac. Many suggestions were made amongst ourselves privately, but it was not until a week before the actual day that we were officially informed of what was being done.

The men of my Company were used on the Beach as a fatigue party for loading stores. We did this work for a few days until the time came for making a final move — and then the whole Truth became known. <u>Every article that could not be carried away had to be destroyed.</u> From the newest rifles and bombs to the oldest jar of Rum; all these things had to be destroyed so that nothing of any value could be left behind for the comfort or use of the Turks.

So, the terrible waste began. At one particular spot, some hundreds of gallons of RUM and WHISKY were drained into the gullies. Our rations of the best quality of tinned sausages, fowl, tongue, ham, various fruits (as well as all kinds of the most delicious biscuits) had to be burned.

During those last few days spent on Gallipoli, the living was excellent. Boxes of "Maconichies Rations" found their way into all the dugouts, and we lived in the lap of luxury. An extra issue of Rum was handed out, which put new life into our hard-working lads. A special shelf had to be dug into the walls of our little earthen homes — which then began to look like small supply-depots.

Our dugouts were well-underground, anything from five to ten feet deep, and neatly-made. A dugout resembles a small room for two, with a few photos and mirrors hanging on the wall to give it a homely appearance. My dugout was only 200 yards from the Naval gun, "Long Tom"; so called because of its extra length and deafening report. I tried several times to get a photo of "Long Tom" in action, and also a photo of the blowing-up of "Long Tom" before we left; but it took our engineers three attempts before "Long Tom" was finally destroyed.

For the last time I studied the rugged hillsides (which had once been thickly- covered with short scrubby bushes of a prickly nature). After the Landing these slopes had soon been cleared; and now there were properly-constructed roads, paths, stables, stores and convenient rooms for the mules' attendants. At night-time, it had the appearance of a hillside village, with lights shining from each house.

I will now relate to you the manner of destroying any stores that could be of benefit to the enemy. All the articles were very carefully stacked in piles near the beach and within easy reach of the Naval guns. Thus, after the evacuation was completed, the ships would fire a few shells into these stockpiles; thereby causing fires that would reduce articles to useless ashes.

Before I could leave this old piece of land known as Anzac, we had to wait a few hours for the lighters to arrive. There were only a few thousand of us gathered at the Pier on the night of December 18th, We were awaiting our turn for embarkation. We were allowed the privilege of relaxing on a small piece of ground between two very high cliffs so that we were sheltered from shell-fire, but not from the straggling bullets which continually buzzed over our heads.

I am pleased to say that no-one was hit. At last the order was given to 'take to the boats', and we had to leave our place of shelter. The men were moved off in groups of 10 and told to march quickly along the pier and get into the lighter. The pier was about 66 yards in length and had a shrapnel shelter along its full length on the "Beachy Bill" side, so we felt partially safe.

After boarding the lighter we had to wait ten minutes for our full complement of men. Those minutes seemed like hours — for the very spot upon which we were floating was within easy range of "Beachy Bill". It proved a very strenuous time because a lighter, when it is fully-loaded, holds about 300 men and "Beachy Bill's" shrapnel contains 300 bullets — that would be exactly one bullet for each of us. What a prize for the enemy!

However, owing to the utmost secrecy and discipline on our part, the Turks did not fire a shot until two days after we had all left the Peninsula. Only when Abdul eventually became suspicious, did "Beachy Bill" begin to shell our piers.

Each night from December 18th. to December 20th. our

evacuation proceeded without interruptions from Abdul. During all this movement, our aeroplanes were very busily engaged in patrol work over our Front-lines. As many as five planes at a time could be seen in operation; and, at the same time, our Destroyers were busily engaged in patrol work along the Beaches.

At night-time, many streamers from the Navy's powerful searchlights were constantly playing upon both flanks of our enemy, making it impossible for the Turks to approach our lines, or to reinforce their own lines, except with great difficulty.

As our lighter steamed away from Anzac, we passed many crafts (Sweepers, Destroyers and Cruisers) and once aboard the KINGSTONIA we looked back and saw a huge fire raging near William's Pier. It was a heap of foodstuffs and clothing that had been left there until the end of the evacuation; but somehow it had become ignited too soon. "Beachy Bill" probably thought his shells had been effective and that <u>he</u> was responsible for this huge blaze.

A Turkish aeroplane actually flew over the pier, making a very close examination of what was happening; but, evidently, he misinterpreted our movements, as the next day the Turks were very busy putting out barbed-wire entanglements, fearing an attack by us. Yet, in reality, each night meant another ten to twelve thousand less men for the Turks to attack.

I must now add a word of praise to those boys who formed the skeleton defence line to safeguard the departure of their comrades. They could only allow two men to guard each 100 yards of trench-lines, and these gallant boys remained until the very last moment; and then made their way down to the water to evacuate the Gallipoli Peninsula, the last ones leaving Anzac at 4.10 a.m. on 20th. December.

Though the Turks may have had some doubts, they did not even once make an attempt to come and see for themselves what we were doing. It was not until two days after our evacuation that they opened up with a terrific Bombardment and followed it with an advance upon our lines — only to find no resistance and EMPTY trenches!

But they found many friendly letters left behind by the Anzacs who commended the Turks for being brave and clever fighters. These letters told them not to think that our evacuation was defeat, but that we had only left to get in first at some other important spot; and that we looked forward to meeting them again in another place and at another time.

In a conspicuous part of a trench at Walker's Ridge, someone had left a good phonograph that was set to play. It had in position a disk entitled "Turkish Patrol" — all it wanted was for someone to set it going and the Turks would hear their own favourite tune."

BACK IN EGYPT AT THE BEGINNING OF 1916

Nelson Langley — Hugh Chaplin H. V. Sleep (England)

In this letter to his mother who lives in Birchip. <u>Private J. D. Green</u> describes the <u>evacuation</u> from Gallipoli.

<u>EGYPT</u>.

<u>January 1916</u>.

"It was a splendidly organised retreat, and great praise is due to the officers for the way in which they planned and carried it out. Every man wanted to be in the rear guard, and it fell to our Battalion to form most of it. 'B' company was placed to cover the rear, and my company was placed in the forks of gullies which all ran into the big one called "Rest Gully". It has high points all round it, and blockades of sand-bags and barbed wire were erected there.

Every man was on the alert, and at dusk every light went out. It was a long night — no noise or smoking was permitted. At last, word was passed along for all men to stand ready; and then the roll was called, and answered in a whisper with the one word, "Yes!" Only <u>120</u> out of <u>260</u> of our company answered to their names. Then came the order to move to embarkation points.

Men had been chosen who were to shoot any stragglers, as it was rumoured there were spies about and the officers were taking no chances of our movements becoming known, or any of our men being shot by snipers. Then we were marched off. It was far more dangerous than in the trenches, as we had to move under the fire of the Turkish artillery guns which always played on the beach.

Our officers now showed their efficiency by marching us among the hills and under cover of our saps, so that near the end of the journey we only had 150 yards of open ground to cross to reach the boat which was to take us off. We heard the report of their guns as our last man slipped on board.

Shells were falling on the new pier that had been erected to take us off, but our officers had decided to take us by the old pier which had previously been almost blown away. The trick worked, and we got off without a man getting a scratch.

Prior to embarking, an order came for all married men to fall in on the left; and we then knew that the rest of us had to stay behind and guard the gullies — with the risk of having to face thousands of Turks at any moment I can tell you that no one was sorry when the last man had safely left.

The day the Turks gave us the big bombardment with

heavy guns was terrible. It lasted for two hours, and it is impossible for you to picture what it was like unless you were there. Scores were not hurt, but to see the dead, wounded and dying men was awful."

[It seems incredible that the Turk did not suspect our troops were leaving Gallipoli, but a trick was played upon them. General White had a brilliant idea (later called the SILENT BATTLE) which was to accustom the Turks to "periods of silence". His plan was put into action from 6 p.m. on November 24th. until midnight on November 27th. At first, this "silent treatment" made the Turks very uneasy and they sent out patrols to reconnoitre. But when their patrols were shot and killed, the Turks realised that the Anzacs were still there, ever-watchful and alert. Conesquently, the Turks put down this unaccustomed silence from the Anzac trenches to "winter preparations". After all, both sides had suffered from the severe storms of November when fierce gales had wrecked ships and piers, and when heavy rains had rushed down the hillsides, filling trenches and drowning men of both armies. Therefore, the Turks, while busy digging in for winter, thought the Anzacs were doing exactly the same.]

GOODBYE, GALLIPOLI!

Private G. A. Mills (*of St. Arnaud writes from Lemnos Island, after the Evacuation, to tell his sister about his recent experiences.*

<u>January, 1916.</u>

"We have left the trenches in Gallipoli, where for a while matters were exciting. I was blown over with a bomb once; hit on the head with a bullet another time (but it was only on top and just cut through my scalp) ; and I was buried by an 8-inch shell another time.

That all happened within the same week! A few days afterwards a piece of shell landed on my coat tail. I was lying on my back, reading, when a big jagged lump of shell dropped.

On another occasion I had just taken my men off the post and was a few yards away when I heard an explosion, and on going to investigate I noticed that our post had been blown down and our ammunition and bombs scattered everywhere. It would have killed some of us for certain if we had been posted.

Water was very scarce and I slept in my clothes and equipment every night. Syd and Tom came here and had a dose of shell-fire and were sent back to Egypt (suffering from shell-shock). Hard luck for them, wasn't it?

Our lads and the Turks had a bit of fun just before the end. We threw tins of beef into their trenches, and they threw cigarettes at us. By the aid of an interpreter, we had a confabulation. We asked them to surrender, but they politely declined!"

Hand-embroidered card

UNLUCKIEST SOLDIER

Private Raymond Charles Bennett (8th. Battalion) of Birchip has always been regarded by his family as a very unlucky soldier because he was shot on the very last day of the evacuation from Gallipoli.

He was rolling up his pack ready to follow his mates down to the beach where ships were waiting for them when suddenly a stray bullet from the Turkish machine guns went through his shoulder and out through his neck.

He was carried from the trench down to the beach and put

on the hospital ship "Devanha" — but he died at 5-30 p.m. before reaching the island of Mudros and was buried at sea. His name is commemorated on the Lone Pine Memorial at Gallipoli.

He enlisted at Birchip on the 1st May, 1915, when he was eighteen — the son of Charles Henry and Mary Jane Bennett. His brother, Edwin Harry Bennett, also enlisted and was a sergeant with the 58th. Battalion until the end of the war.

Mrs. Gilbert of Chirrup received the following news from her son <u>Private Fred Gilbert.</u>

<u>December 25th. 1915.</u>

"I am in splendid health. I received your two Xmas boxes on December 18th. and I can tell you that after eight weeks in the trenches on bully beef, biscuits and rice, I enjoyed the plum duff and Xmas cake immensely. Needless to say, I never wasted any time in devouring them. I expected to spend Xmas in the trenches amidst the bursting shrapnel, but instead of that we are spending it in Lemnos Island — out of the sound of guns and under a beautiful cloudless sky.

Football is in full swing, with everyone enjoying themselves, for the day at least. War and all its horrors are banished from our minds, and mirth and merriment prevail. By the time this letter arrives, you will have read all about our evacuation of Gallipoli. It was splendidly carried out. The 14th. Battalion is now on its way to Egypt — but where our next move will be we do not know.

The peninsula was a very cold part of the world, but very healthy, as during the two months I was there I never saw a man suffering from a cold. The life of a soldier agrees with me. I am getting as fat as a pig, never had a day's sickness, and never felt better in my life. Ray Bennett, from Birchip, was wounded on the evening we left the peninsula. He was rolling up his pack, ready to move off, when a bullet plugged him under the shoulder and came out by his neck."

[*Rau Bennett, poor chap, later died from his wound. He was certainly unlucky to be hit by a stray bullet during the evacuation. About 36,000 troops were successfully removed from under the very noses of the Turks. This gradual withdrawal commenced on the 8th. December; yet the men themselves were unaware of what was happening, or where they were being taken. They were given strict orders to fall in, and be completely quiet. Socks, or sandbags, were wrapped around their boots to deaden the sound of movement on rocks and pebbles. As the men filed down Gallipoli's slopes to the beaches, their eyes looked back at the hills where they had buried their mates and they were reluctant to leave them. Silently, except for an occasional oath as someone stumbled in the dark, soldiers filed along the beach and then were squashed like sardines into the naval barges.*]

TROOPER ALFRED BAILES

Another soldier who enlisted in Donald — although born in Richmond — was Alfred Bailes and he became one of the 60,000 Australians who died in that Great War (1914-18). His mother drowned when Alfred was young and he was put into an orphanage. At the age of 17 he was sent from Melbourne to work on the estate of William Pope, at Cope Cope, near Donald.

When the war came, Alf enlisted in November, 1914. He was a natural warrior, blessed with the shooting and survival skills of a bushman and as a perfect specimen of Australian youth, Alf was accepted at once because this country was keen to send her best men to help in Britain's conflict.

He named his employer (W. R. Pope) as his 'next-of-kin' on the enlistment papers. Alf was then 26 years old and he was 5ft.-9ins tall. As an excellent rider, he was able to pass the difficult tests to become a Trooper in the Light Horse Regiment.

Alfred Bailes embarked on 'HMT Wiltshire' (13th. April, 1915) to sail to Egypt where they trained on the desert sands, but instead of going to France, he was sent to Gallipoli with other Light-Horse men to help the Infantry who had suffered great losses since the Landing sadly, it meant leaving their horses behind in Egypt and going into the trenches. Alfred was killed on the 8th. August, 1915, in that terrible <u>slaughter at the Nek, and is buried with many others in the Beach Cemetery.</u>

The cross bears the inscription -

IN MEMORY OF TROOPER ALFRED BAILES.

4TH L. H. R.

KILLED IN ACTION.

7/8/1915.

AGED 28 YEARS.

Our late comrade was buried in what is known to us as the Beach Cemetery"

A GALLIPOLI MAN LOOKS BACK

"I joined the army on August 12th. (which was the eve of my 21st. birthday) and was assigned to the 8th. Victorian Battalion (2nd. Infantry Brigade). After only six weeks' training at Broadmeadows Camp in Melbourne, we left for Western Australia to become part of the 20,000 Australians and 10,000 New Zealanders who formed the First Convoy.

I shall never forget that majestic sight, on October 31st. in King George's Sound, as we waited to set sail. There were 40 transports lying at anchor on that broad expanse of water outside Albany — and we were guarded by 8 warships which were to escort and protect us.

Our great fleet sailed away on November 1st. (1914) for Egypt; and the only outstanding event of that journey was the Sydney-Emden fight near the Cocos Islands (which we did not actually see). We arrived in Egypt on December 7th. and camped just under the Pyramids.

After months of training in the desert, we went to Lemnos Island, close to the Dardanelles Straits and the Gallipoli Peninsula. We still did not know where we were going but we had to practice climbing up and down rope-ladders attached to ships; so we got the idea we were going to land somewhere!

The landing came on April 25th. We were told to be ready by 3 a.m. and everyone was issued with 48 hours rations. We were told not to make any noise when we neared the shore because the idea was to take the Turks by surprise.

The strong currents took our boats further north than the intended landing-place and so we landed in daylight and copped everything the Turks had to throw at us; machine-guns, rifles, the lot. We copped a terrible lot of casualties.

They seemed to pick off all our officers; I think it was because they wore belts with shiny brass buckles, making them perfect targets for Turkish snipers.

April 25th. was a day of carnage and confusion. We scaled the Gallipoli Heights and my Battalion (8th.) found itself on the extreme right flank in a far-flung position, appropriately named "Tasmania Post".

We were given orders to dig in. I was on the shovel and a fellow named Fred Adams was on the pick. He got shot through the forehead and died instantly. The Turks attacked us all through the night. They said they were going to drive us back into the sea, but they never did.

The living-conditions were shocking. Our water came all the way from Egypt in fuel tins and was tainted with petrol; and all of us were hit with dysentery. Because of the water shortage, tea had to be boiled in dirty pans and it tasted like poison.

Lice was a terrible problem. I can remember my mate, George, and I were covered with them. They used to crawl up the sides of our tent and drop on us. The Aegean Sea was our only relief from these parasites; yet it was not really safe to go for a swim because shells landed frequently on the little beach.

One day George and I went for a swim to get clean; and while we were swimming there, bullets from a mile away were hitting the water. We also had to watch out for "Beachy Bill" (our nickname for a particular Turkish gun which fired high-explosive shells into the beach vicinity).

I remember there were two other blokes lying naked in the sun, in a rocky alcove further up the beach. All of a sudden there was a massive explosion, and I said to my mate, George, "The next one will be for us, let's get going". The shell had hit the rocky alcove, and all that was left of those poor men were bits of flesh hanging from the walls. We got back up Shrapnel Gully as quick as we could move.

About a week later I had another lucky escape, but George (Killingbeck) was not so fortunate. A shell from a German warship hit our underground tunnel. Three of my mates were killed and George staggered out with his arm hanging by two threads. If I'd been in there, I'd have copped it, too; but something told me to go and make a cup of tea, and so I was outside when the shell hit.

George was so badly wounded that it looked as though he would die. He recovered after a series of operations in England. The next time I saw him was after the war when I bumped into him at Caulfield Races. He'd lost his arm, his left eye, and had a hole in his leg. We kept in touch till George died in 1980.

At the beginning of May, my 8th.Battalion was sent to help the British Forces at Cape Helles. The aim was to drive inland and capture the town of Krithia. The assault started about 4 p.m. and it was impossible to 'dig-in' because the ground was like concrete. We passed two British regiments and they were yelling, "Go on, Aussies, go on!"

But we didn't get very far. We advanced 1000 yards and

then we were slaughtered. They took a roll call next morning and from 900 men we only had 200 left.

Then we were sent to Lemnos island for a badly-needed rest before going into action again at "Lone Pine". It was here that I saw how Simpson got his donkey. This chap and I were on observation-post duty when we noticed some Indian soldiers set up a mountain-gun above us and start firing it at the Turks. But the Turks blew those Indians to pieces. The donkeys that had carried the gun up the hill now wandered off because they had lost their guides.

One of these donkeys was later found by Simpson who kept it in his possession. Private John Simpson Kirkpatrick became a legendary character when he used this same donkey to carry wounded soldiers down the steep cliffs to Anzac Cove for medical treatment. After several weeks with the donkey, Simpson was killed by a sniper as he travelled along Shrapnel Gully.

Gallipoli ended for me in August, 1915, when I was suffering from dysentery and other ailments. They sent me to England where I carried out light duties till the end of the war.

The Allied forces were withdrawn from Gallipoli in December, 1915. They said the evacuation was the most successful operation of the entire campaign, carried out with the loss of only three lives. In those eight months there, both sides had suffered more than half a million casualties.

The Australians lost 7,818 men, with 19,511 wounded. I think it was the biggest mistake ever made. We should never have gone to Gallipoli. No wonder when Lord Kitchener came to the Peninsula to look over the campaign, he said we were to get out straight away."

BILL GROVES (Melbourne)

Using a periscope in the trenches
A long, hollow box with a mirror fixed at both ends

FINAL THOUGHTS OF GALLIPOLI

As soon as the boats touched bottom our boys threw off their packs, jumped into the sea, fixed bayonets and charged. God, when I think of that Hell. "THOU SHALT DO NO MURDER" says the Good Book.

The foe did not wait for a closer acquaintance but fled. However, in the light of after-events, I'm inclined to believe this was only a ruse to entice our fellows into a position from which they could be put out of action.

Our lads, glorious lads, were very eager to get up to closer quarters with the enemy — and they had their wish soon enough. Our fellows were subjected to a murderous fire from shrapnel, rifles and machine-guns, and could for the most part only lie, helpless, under cover.

Attacks would be thrown forward, under cover of supporting fire from their comrades, whose remnants would then have to retire with great loss of life. Finally, a defensive position was taken up along the ridges a little over a mile from the sea, and trenches hastily dug.

The enemy gunners had our ranges marked out, and worked havoc amongst us with their shrapnel. In the afternoon a critical moment arrived, and for a time it seemed as if the Australians would be beaten back into the sea. But the dauntless spirits of the officers and N.C.O's. kept the men from becoming panic-stricken, and with the approach of darkness came a cessation of the shrapnel fire which had been so demoralising.

As Sherman said, "WAR IS HELL". Many of the wounded lay all night, unattended, owing to the number of stretchers being absolutely inadequate to cope with the great number of casualties.

It was pathetic to see the wounded wending their way down to the beach. I noticed a large percentage were wounded in the arms, so these found no difficulty in walking to the beach, but the more severe cases crawled out of the firing-line on hands and knees, many to die on the way.

Shame on those who say the Australian is a waster! Even if the most noted gambler and drunkard in Australia is in our ranks, take your hat off to him when he returns, for he deserves all the honor Australians can offer — and more!

The Turks advanced to the attack on the following day with renewed vigour, but by this time our bonny boys had entrenched themselves, and were supported by the guns of the warships and the Indian Mountain Battery. The Australians then repelled many attacks.

The fire from the field guns is too awful to describe. When the shell explodes in the air, small leaden balls are broadcast over an area of 25 yards wide by 200 yards long. Most wounds were caused by shrapnel — and the wound made by it is most horrible.

I have seen some fearful cases. One of my dearest pals had his leg blown off at the knee. Nothing could be done for him. I stood beside him, held his hand, and watched him die in awful agony. Then I — stern-hearted William Fry — burst into tears.

Yes, I cried as I never had since childhood, touched by the awful death of a true Australian in a strange land. God, this is war!

One noticeable feature about the Turk is his penchant for employing all sorts of underhand methods in order to achieve an object. Sniping is his favourite plan of attack.

The Turks secrete themselves in dug-outs on the hillsides, and at every favourable opportunity shoot our fellows.

When caught they receive short shrift, as our men are greatly incensed at this despicable mode of fighting.

I was not in action long before I committed my first murder; yes, MURDER — what else can I call it ? My mate was killed by one of those Turkish gentry, so I waited till the sniper showed himself 50 yards away.

Click! My bullet carried true and there was another widow in Turkey. My mate's death was avenged — and thus I commenced a murderous career. I have now killed too many to remember their number.

(Cpl. W. Fry was shot through the head by a Turkish sniper whilst on duty with General Bridges who was also fatally wounded soon afterwards.)

CONCLUSION

THE WINTER OF 1915 AT GALLIPOLI

The hurricanes which raged from November 27th. to the 29th. were a terrible trial, imprisoning troops in their narrow ridges and trenches. In rained in torrents for twelve hours and then a piercing frost froze their drenched overcoats so stiff that they stood up by themselves. The water froze men's feet as they slept from sheer exhaustion. After the frost came a blizzard — so the men, frozen and buffeted by the wind and sleet, were hardly able to move and keep their circulation going.

The sentries who were watching at the loopholes were frozen to death. They were found dead at their posts, frozen rigid, their fingers still clutching their rifles in an iron grip. When a 12-hour rain came after a cloud burst, it turned the gullies into raging torrents. Dead bodies of drowned Turks were washed down the hillside with carcasses of mules. The trenches were flooded so quickly that soldiers on both sides were drowned.

GALLIPOLI.

From April to December the Allied Forces hung on till orders came from London to withdraw. On 19th. December the last of the Australians and New Zealanders were evacuated from Gallipoli for Egypt. By then 7,600 Aussies and 2,500 New Zealanders had been killed — and 19,000 Aussies and 5,000 New Zealanders had been wounded. We should remember that French casualties were just as high as those of the Anzacs — and the British lost nearly three times as many.

THE LANDING AT GALLIPOLI became known as ANZAC DAY for it symbolized the noblest military operation of this country's people and created a bond for men who had been through that fiery furnace.

The winter months brought icy winds and heavy falls of snow that sometimes lasted for three days, so the men began suffering from frost-bite. By the last week in November the Anzacs' trenches were so full of snow, rain and mud that deaths from exposure numbered about 200 — and men on both sides drowned in their flooded trenches. Then during the first week in December over 10,000 sick British soldiers were removed by hospital ships.

Therefore, it was finally decided to evacuate all troops and leave Gallipoli to the Turks and to the awful weather. Since the Landing, 7,594 Australians and 2,431 New Zealanders had died; and although Turkey won the Peninsula War over 66,000 of her own soldiers had been killed.

The first Anzacs were successfully shipped away on the 13th. December and by the 16th. December the number left in their trenches was reduced to 20,000 whilst the enemy lines opposite were held by 170,000 men. Fortunately, the Turks never knew about this state of affairs.

It was the 19th. December when the last Anzacs left Gallipoli, yet still the enemy was completely unaware of that British Evacuation, such was its great speed and silent execution.

Thus, Gallipoli remained in the hands of the Turks and Britain's campaign to capture the Straits was a failure. Yet those 10,000 Australian and New Zealand soldiers did not die in vain because they died for their country, defending its freedom and justice.

How did 22,000 men manage to shuffle downhill in the light of a full moon and then assemble on the exposed beaches ready to clamber aboard their ships without alerting the Turks perched on cliffs directly above them? It was thanks to a brilliant invention by a young soldier, Bill Scurry, who designed a way to make rifles fire on their own by using water and tin cans thus making the enemy think our soldiers were still in their trenches.

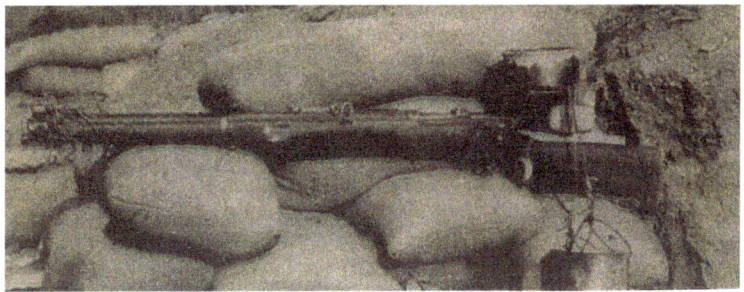

FINISHED

After six months of heavy fighting only the fringe of the coastline had been secured by the Allies; whilst the Turks still commanded the highest positions along that inhospitable Peninsula. Then winter arrived near the end of 1915 and during the last week in November torrential rain fell everywhere, followed by heavy frost and blizzards so that all the trenches were full of snow, rain and mud. Deaths from exposure numbered about 200 and over 10,000 sick soldiers were taken away by the beginning of December. Thus it was decided to evacuate all troops and leave Gallipoli to the Turks.

The first men were taken off on December 13th. and by the 16th. December the number of Anzacs was reduced to 20,000 whilst the enemy trenches opposite were held by 170,000 men. (If the Turks only knew.) By the 19th. December the last Anzacs left Gallipoli and still the enemy was unaware of the evacuation such was the great success of its execution.

So Gallipoli remained in the hands of the Turks and the campaign to capture the Straits was a failure. But who shall say that **10,000** Australian and New Zealand soldiers who died a hero's death on those bullet-swept heights and shell-blitzed beaches gave their lives in vain?

Types Of The British Army.

THE UNBURIED DEAD

By the way, did you know that the Turks never had time to bury their dead when the Gallipoli Campaign was finished?

For years, the remains of both British and Turkish soldiers were left unburied and uncollected across that wild and desolate Peninsula.

One old digger visiting Gallipoli in 1963 wrote: PECULIAR FEELINGS AROSE IN MY HEART WHEN I SAW THE MANY HUMAN SKULLS AND LARGE BONES JUST LYING AROUND EXPOSED TO THE ELEMENTS.

Although that was 48 years after the campaign, yet human remains were still scattered over the Peninsula.

When the War Graves Commission sent burial parties to Gallipoli in 1920 they were surprised to see what looked like painted white lines up and down the hillsides — they

273

went closer and found those lines were made by the bleached bones of fallen soldiers.

DISTRICT SOLDIERS
WHO DIED AT GALLIPOLI

L/Cpl. James Alfred ANDERSON (8th. Light Horse Regiment) was killed in that suicidal attack on the Nek (7th. August) when four lines of the 8th. and 10th. Light Horsemen were ordered to attack and each line was mown down as soon as they left their trenches.

Trooper Alfred BAILES (4th. Light Horse Regiment) was also killed in action on that terrible slaughter at the Nek (7th. August) and is buried with many others in the Beach Cemetery.

Trooper Alexander Andrews (Wattie) BARBER (8th. Light Horse Regiment) died from his wounds on 22nd. June, 1915, after a hand grenade burst beside him and pieces of shrapnel hit his head, arms, hands, stomach and legs. He suffered for six hours before succumbing to his terrible wounds.

Private Raymond Charles BENNETT (14th. Battalion) may have been the last soldier to be killed on Gallipoli Heights because he was rolling up his pack ready to be evacuated on December 18th. when a stray Turkish bullet entered his chest and through his neck he died on a hospital ship and was buried at sea.

Private James BOOLEY (14th. Battalion) was killed in action on 8th. August, 1915, in that brave attack on Turkish positions at 'Lone Pine'. Before enlisting he worked for many years on the Donald Railway as a train shunter.

Trooper Walter COOMBS, a veteran of the South African War (1899-1902), joined the 8th. Light Horse Regiment at the beginning of World War 1. He was shot down by the Turks during the Landing on the Gallipoli Peninsula — 25th. April, 1915.

Private James Wilkie McJUNKIN (6th.Battalion) was wounded on Bolton's Ridge and his left leg was amputated — but he died from his wounds on a hospital ship on the 5th. May, 1915, and was buried at sea. (Before enlisting he had worked on a local newspaper and became a journalist.)

Private Clifford POLKINGHORNE (8th. Battalion) was killed on the 25th. April, 1915, in action during the fighting that followed the landing. His brother, Reginald Clyde Polkinghorne describes in his letter how Clifford was shot in the back when Turks disguised in the uniforms of dead Australians crept up behind them.

Sapper Edward Albert George ROGASCH was killed on 27th. June, 1915, whilst in a tunnel that was being dug under No Man's Land at Lone Pine. The Turks exploded two mines nearby, and so the tunnel collapsed, burying him alive.

Private William Henry TRACY (7th. Battalion) was first wounded during the landing on 25th. April as he sat in a boat being rowed to shore. A bullet entered his back and lodged in his lung — but after his recovery in Egypt he returned to Gallipoli and there was killed in action on 8th. August, 1915, in the fierce battle at Lone Pine when he was blown to bits by a bomb that fell into his trench.

TO THOSE HEROES WHO SHED THEIR BLOOD AND LOST THEIR LIVES YOU ARE NOW LYING IN THE SOIL OF A FRIENDLY COUNTRY SO REST IN PEACE

YOU THE MOTHERS WHO SENT THEIR SONS FROM FAR AWAY COUNTRIES WIPE AWAY YOUR TEARS AS YOUR SONS ARE NOW LYING IN OUR BOSOM AND AT PEACE HAVING LOST THEIR LIVES ON THIS LAND THEY HAVE BECOME OUR SONS AS WELL.

Simpson and his donkey rescue wounded soldiers (Melbourne Shrine)

A GRATEFUL NATION

Give thanks! Give thanks!, Australia, for all your heroes great,
Who fought advancing fearlessly across that bloody strait;
Up hills where death their glory tells
Mown down upon the Dardanelles.
Give thanks! Give thanks! Australia, for sons who proved their worth
Whom Turk and Hun, unmerciful, shot down on foreign earth.
Let not some thoughtless youth despise that sacrifice of noble lives
Whose blood was spilt 'neath Turkish skies.
No other deed can now out-shine that Landing on Gallipoli Heights
Though deadly showers of bullets met them there, they stayed for
many nights.
With cold, hard steel they forged a way 'till seas turned red with
blood that day
And bodies floated in the bay.
Do not forget, Australia, each torn and tortured son,
But give him thanks his wounds deserve for loyal duty done.
Do not forget our Anzacs brave, whose deeds of valour history tells
Upon the deadly Dardanelles.
— Florence Breed

DIGGING GRAVES

NO LOVE CAN EVER GIVE WHAT THEIR LIFE HAS OFFERED US BY YIELDING IN A MOMENT ALL THE DAYS AND YEARS IT HAD BEFORE IT.

NO SACRIFICE IS COMPARABLE WITH THAT WHICH THEY HAVE OFFERED US.

THAT IS WHY THERE IS NO GLORY THAT CAN ATTAIN TO THEIRS, NO GRATITUDE GREATER THAN THAT WHICH WE OWE TO THEM.

(Maurice Maeterlinck)

Photo: Gunner Jack Whittaker

"The Australian and New Zealand troops have indeed proved themselves worthy sons of the Empire."

GEORGE R.I.

Pte L. McConechy

Pte A. Bailes

By that time 7,594 Australians and 2,431 New Zealanders had died and although Turkey won the Peninsula War, over 66,000 of her soldiers had been killed.

Pte J. Hoare

L/CpL J W Walder

THE KAISER'S DREAM

(written by Unknown Soldier)

There's a story now current, though strange it may seem,
Of the great Kaiser Bill and his wonderful dream.
Being tired of his allies he laid down in bed
And amongst other things he dreamt he was dead.
In a very fine coffin and lying-in-state,
With a guard of brave Germans who mourned for his fate.
He wasn't long dead when he found to his cost
That his soul outside a body was feeling quite lost.
On leaving this earth to Heaven he went straight
And arriving up there gave a knock at the gate.
But St. Peter looked out and with voice loud and clear
Said, "Begone, Kaiser Bill, we don't want you here!"
"Well," said the Kaiser, "that's very uncivil
I suppose after this I must go to the Devil."
So he turned on his heel and off he did go
At the top of his speed to the regions below.
But when he got there he was filled with dismay
For whilst waiting outside he heard Old Nick say
To his Imps, "Now look here, boys, I give you a warning
I'm expecting the Kaiser down here in the morning,
But don't let him in, for to me it's quite clear
He's a very bad man, so we don't want him here.
For once he gets in there'll be no end of quarrels,
In fact, I'm afraid he'll corrupt our good morals."
"O Satan, dear friend," the Kaiser then cried,
"Excuse me for listening while waiting outside.

If you don't let me in, then where can I go?"
"Indeed," said the Devil, "I really don't know!"
"Oh, please let me in, I'm feeling quite cold,"
Said the Kaiser, quite anxious to enter Nick's fold.
"Let me sit in a comer, no matter how hot."
"No," said the Devil, "most certainly not!
We don't admit people for riches, or help.
Here's sulphur and matches, make Hell for yourself."
They kicked 'Old Bill' out, then vanished in smoke
And just at that moment the Kaiser awoke.
He jumped out of bed in a shivering sweat
And said, "Well, that dream I shall never forget.
That I can't go to Heaven I know very well,
But it's really too bad to be kicked out of Hell."

*(This poem, printed on a penny postcard,
was sent home by soldiers.)*

Over the years there have been many speculations about which Australian soldiers had the record for certain actions.

Who was the <u>FIRST</u> Anzac to step ashore on the Gallipoli Peninsula at the beginning of that sea-borne invasion of Turkey? It was <u>Sergeant Joseph Stratford</u>, killed in action on April 25th. 1915, because on a church plaque in Lismore (where he had lived) is written, "<u>Eyewitnesses state that he was the first Australian to land at Gallipoli.</u>" Apparently, several returned Victorian soldiers gave evidence to prove he was the first!

Who was the <u>YOUNGEST</u> Anzac? It was <u>James Charles Martin</u>, only 14, but he had persuaded his mother to give her permission for him to enlist. He left with the 21st. Battalion and was heading for Gallipoli on the 'Southland' when she was torpedoed and so he spent many hours in the freezing water with many others until rescued. He did not reach Gallipoli until September — which was the beginning of winter there. It was a fact that by then it was not so much the Turks but flooded trenches and diseases that were killing soldiers. Sadly, Martin contracted typhoid fever and died on a hospital ship just three months short of his 15th. Birthday.

Who was the LAST Anzac killed at Gallipoli? This record probably belongs to a local District soldier, <u>Private Raymond Charles Bennett</u>. He was very unlucky because as he was leaving his trench during the evacuation — and walking behind a long line of soldiers on their way down to the rescue ships — a stray Turkish bullet hit him. He died on a hospital ship and was buried at sea.

L — R: Joseph Stratford and James Martin

Was he really the first Anzac to step ashore on the Gallipoli Peninsula at the beginning of that sea-borne invasion of Turkey?

SERGEANT JOSEPH STRATFORD's parents received a telegram stating their son had been killed in action on April 25, 1915 and a returned Victorian soldier gave evidence that Sgt. Stratford was the first, man to land. On a church plaque in Lismore is written. "Eyewitnesses state that he was the first Australian to land at Gallipoli."

CAPTAIN ALFRED SHOUT and six other Australians were awarded the Victoria Cross tor their brave actions at the Battle of Lone Pine in August, 1915. It was on the 9th. August during a counter-attack on the enemy trenches that Captain Sasse and his friend, Captain Shout, led their men along a trench —
and whilst Sasse was shooting, Shout was bombing. But when

Shout lit three bombs at once in a final dash, the last bomb burst in his hand, destroying one side of his body.

CORPORAL ALEXANDER BURTON was awarded the Victoria Cross for conspicuous bravery during the fighting at Lone Pine on August 9th. when the Turks made a counter-attack upon a newly-captured enemy trench held by Cpl Burton, Lt. Tubb and Cpl. Dunstan. The Turks blew down their sandbag barricade, but the three men repulsed them and rebuilt it. Three times the enemy blew down their barricade, but each time they were driven off. Burton was killed by a bomb whilst building up the barricade.

JAMES CHARLES MARTIN at 14 perhaps looked old for his age, but anyone under 21 required parental permission to enlist. However, he persuaded his mother to give her permission and later left with the 21st Infantry Battalion aboard the 'Berrima' on June 28th. 1915. He was heading for Gallipoli on the transport ship 'Southland' when she was torpedoed and Martin with many others spent hours in the water until rescued, and so he did not reach Gallipoli until September. By then it was not so much the Turks but diseases that were killing men. Martin contracted typhoid fever and died on a. hospital ship, just three months short, of his 15th. Birthday.

COLLECTING BONES
FROM ANZAC COVE

'POMPEY' ELLIOTT

By the time World War 1 ended on November 11, 1918, about 60,000 Australians had lost their lives whilst others returned home suffering from injuries, both physical and mental. Many had shell shock ('post traumatic stress syndrome') In those days, few people understood what it meant, even though there were daily tragedies to prove this terrible affliction existed amongst returned soldiers.

Perhaps one of the saddest examples concerns Senator H. E. Elliott who returned safely from the war and became a respected Member of Parliament. As an officer both in Gallipoli and France, Major-General Elliott (nicknamed 'Pompey') was well-liked by his men.

The decisions he had to make in the heat of battle (such as at Lone Pine in Gallipoli, and at Fromelles, on the Western Front) must have tormented his mind. In fact, when Senator Elliott was invited in 1930 to unveil the War Memorial at Ararat, he could not hold back his tears a sure sign he was suffering from horrific wartime memories.

His mental condition reached a climax when he tried to gas himself, so his doctor arranged for Senator Elliott to be under constant supervision at a private hospital in Elsternwick. The nurses took away anything with which he might harm himself, but made the mistake of allowing him to keep his shaving kit.

Using a cut-throat razor, on the morning of the 23rd. March, 1931, Senator Elliott committed suicide by slashing his wrists. He was given a State Funeral and thousands lined the streets to farewell that great soldier and statesman — but the cause of his death was published in the newspapers as 'cerebral haemorrhage' and the real reason for his demise was never mentioned.

Harold (Pompey) Elliot

The Somme mud.

ANZAC — A word invented by an English clerk who was tired of having to write the words 'Australian and New

Zealand Army Corps' on all the mail that passed through his hands. This word not only reminds us of the great loss of men in war, but also of their courage and endurance in the face of adversity; it means a love of one's country and a faithful duty to it; above all, this word represents mateship and good humour in times of great hardship, as well as a sense of self-worth against dreadful odds.

Tyne Cott War Memorial Cemetery — Belgium
(photo D.E.Breed)

GALLIPOLI

One fateful day, long time ago,
Our soldiers faced a foreign foe.
They bravely sailed for several nights
And reached at dawn Gallipoli Heights
They rowed ashore in little boats,
With just their guns and overcoats.
Pell-mell they raced across the sand,
That resolute, courageous band.
The bullets whizzing all around
Felled many soldiers to the ground.
But up steep slopes the remnant dash,
O'er hills they race, and in a flash
Their bayonets scare those Turks on high
Who run away, afraid to die.
Our Anzacs bold have won the day,
So give them praise. But there they stay
For eight long months, and had to suffer
Weevils, wounds and wintry weather.
Oft snipers' bullets took a life,
And so did fever in that strife.
The hills looked like a scene from Hell
With corpses lying where they fell.
When Winter's floods forced a retreat,
Our soldiers left on silent feet.
With aching hearts they said Goodbye
To mates they left 'neath Turkey's sky.

— *Florence Breed*

DEATH TOLL

TURKEY	85,000+
BRITAIN	41,148
FRANCE	9798
AUSTRALIA	8709
NEW ZEALAND	2721
INDIA	1350
NEWFOUNDLAND	49

~ Gallipoli ~

The Landing

THE GRIEVING MOTHER

Holds photo of her dead son close to her heart.

(Statue erected in Ballarat, 2017)

I had no skill to offer

I had no wealth to spend

Mine was a greater glory

I had a son to send

Silently the shades of evening

gather round my lonely door

Silently they bring before me

the face I shall see no more

This life-sized statue (erected in Ballarat in February, 1917) entitled 'Grieving Mother' was created by the eminent sculptor, Peter Corlett, O.A.M., whose famous works include the 'Cobbers' statue at Fromelles, and the 'Simpson and his Donkey' statue at the War Memorial, in Canberra.

The 'Grieving Mother' statue reminds us of the terrible loss of young men when more than 60,000 Australians died in the First World War, far from the land of their birth. What effect did it have upon their loved ones at home?

This impressive statue is an unusual way to commemorate the centenary of that conflict. Records say that of all Australians who went to the war, one in five lost his life; about two in five were wounded; and the remaining two in five returned home badly affected mentally — some committed suicide, or even murder.

The 'Grieving Mother' is holding a photo of her dead son close to her heart — and this is one aspect of the First World War that has never been closely examined — the love of a mother for her lost· son. Can such a cruel bereavement be adequately described in words? The suffering and heartache of a mother after learning that her beloved son had been killed would be heart-rending.

CPSIA information can be obtained
at www.ICGtesting.com
Printed in the USA
BVHW091417091120
592859BV00019B/2088